C000255806

The Boys' Book of Soccer 1966

£3-00

The Boys' Book of Soccer 1966

Edited by Dennis Smith

Evans Brothers Limited, London

This Evans Centenary edition first published 2007
Published by Evans Brothers Ltd
2A Portman Mansions
Chiltern Street
London W1U 6NR

© Evans Brothers Limited 1966

This is a special Evans Centenary facsimile edition of the Boys' Book of Soccer that was first published in 1966. Relive the glorious World Cup summer – Eusebio, the plucky North Koreans, Rattin and the Argentinians in the semi-final against England, and of course the Final – 4:2 to England. Admire the magnificent team including the all-time greats Moore, Charlton, Hurst, Stiles, Ball, and the greatest keeper of them all, Gordon Banks.

On the domestic front, take a trip down Memory Lane to when the English Football League had four divisions, numbered One to Four, and when fans stood to watch their heroes on something called terraces. Brush up on the laws of the game, team colours, and soccer records and celebrities.

Take yourself back to the finest moment in English football's history – it's all here.

Acknowledgements
Photographs reproduced by permission of Express Newspapers, Reuters and Mirrorpix/Action Images. Cartoons by Rich

All rights reserved. No part of this publication may be reproduced, stored in a retrieval system or transmitted, in any form or by any means, electronic, mechanical, photocopying, recording or otherwise, without prior permission of Evans Brothers Limited.

British Library Cataloguing in Publication Data is available for this title.

ISBN 9780237535001

Printed in Malta by Gutenberg Press Ltd.

VISIT OUR WEBSITE
www.evansbooks.co.uk
Evans

Contents

Frontispiece: Bobby Moore's Victory Kiss

West Germany equalise less than a minute from time. *Above:* Emmerich prepares to take the free kick. *Below:* The ball is in the net, with the England defence spreadeagled.
The free kick itself was disputed by the England players, who claimed that Jackie Charlton had headed the ball without committing a foul.

England's Victory in the World Cup

With less than a minute to go before the final whistle, England were leading West Germany 2—1 and seemed certain of winning the World Cup. Then came disaster.

Jackie Charlton was penalised after jumping to a header, and Emmerich took the free kick. The ball went through the defensive wall, cannoned across the face of the goal and Weber banged it into the net. Germany had equalised.

The England team, so close to victory, had to face extra time knowing that their opponents would have the impetus of coming from behind to spur on their weary bodies through another half an hour of gruelling football.

But England did not falter. From the restart they pegged back the Germans in their own half of the field, and soon Alan Ball's powerful drive was just tipped over the bar by goalkeeper Tilkowski. Then Bobby Charlton had a low drive pushed against an upright.

The Germans, tired by their efforts in the first forty-five minutes on the heavy turf, still looked dangerous when they broke away, but the England defence, unchanged for the whole series, was as competent as ever. Two goals had been conceded by them in this game; they were grimly determined that there should be no more.

In the tenth minute of extra time Geoff Hurst took a pass from Ball, worked an opening for himself and sent in a rising shot from ten yards out. The ball was deflected on to the underside of the bar by Tilkowski, and rebounded downwards. The England team appealed for a goal, the Swiss referee appeared to ignore them, and then went over to consult his Russian linesman.

By emphatic nods the linesman indicated that the ball had crossed the line, and the referee pointed to the middle. For the second time England were ahead.

In the last period of extra time the Germans sometimes had seven or eight players in England's penalty area. They risked the break — and paid for it. Bobby Moore, the England skipper, took the ball out of defence in the dying seconds with Hurst on his own ten yards inside the German half. Moore laid on yet another of his wonderfully accurate passes that had been a feature of England's play, and Hurst streaked away. As Tilkowski prepared to move out, Hurst swung his left foot and drove the ball into the top of the net for his side's fourth goal and his own hat-trick. For the first time ever a player had scored three goals in a World Cup-final.

All this after they had been a goal down after ten minutes, when a defensive error by Ray Wilson allowed Haller to shoot past Gordon Banks. England were soon on level terms. Moore flighted a free kick from forty yards out towards the far post, Hurst slipped past the defence, and a perfect header gave the goalkeeper no chance.

It was 1—1 at the interval, and although the Germans looked slightly the better side they had taken more out of themselves. In the second half England began to get on top, but it was not until a quarter of an hour from the end that they got what appeared to be the deciding goal.

Haller (*extreme right*) scores West Germany's first goal.

The ball came over to Hurst on the left, following a corner on the other side, and his shot was deflected across the goal by Schulz, the German 'sweeper'. Martin Peters, unmarked, took it on the half-volley and drove it into the net from five yards.

Then came Weber's dramatic equaliser, and the drama in extra time. England's 4—2 victory was deserved.

In the Final they produced a good deal more flair and determination than in the earlier Rounds, and in so doing they and their sporting opponents brought the competition to a thrilling climax.

Peters (No. 16) scores England's second.

And Geoff Hurst gets a third for England in extra time.

It had opened nearly three weeks earlier with a dreary game between England and Uruguay. England, for the most part, played rigid, unimaginative football, running about feverishly and getting nowhere, while Uruguay, playing for a draw from the start, retreated in depth.

Neither side scored, and there was precious little entertainment.

In the twenty-four Eighth-Final matches in Chile four years before, seventeen teams failed to score. It looked as though the English crowds might have to endure another series in which attacking soccer was at a premium.

But next day the feeble performances of England and Uruguay were to some extent forgotten. Champions Brazil entered the fray, the much-fancied West Germans played their first game, and the unknowns of North Korea took on the might of the Soviet Union.

Brazil's 2–0 victory over Bulgaria had a thoroughly professional look about it, although both goals came from free kicks. Pele, as expected, came in for a number of crunching tackles, and it was from one of them that the first goal came. He took the kick himself, and blasted the ball in from about three yards outside the penalty area.

In the second half, Garrincha, from a little farther out, sent in a vicious, outswinging drive that went over the heads of the wall of defenders, and the Bulgarian goalkeeper was still getting into position when the ball hit the back of the net.

In spite of their victory, however, the champions did not look entirely convincing. Garrincha was slow, and nothing like the player of 1962, the defence showed unmistakable signs of age, and they already had a formidable list of injured players, including Zito and Amarildo. Their one hope, the genius Pele, was obviously going to be so closely marked in every game that his chance of going through the competition unscathed looked remote.

The Bulgarians had two fine forwards in Asparuhov and Yakimov, but finding themselves in the best footballing group that included Hungary and Portugal as well as the champions they looked to have no chance of further progress.

Meanwhile the West Germans had put five into the Swiss net without reply. The Swiss, tidy and industrious in all they did but rather lucky to reach the last sixteen, were no match for their opponents. The dynamism of Schnellinger ruled the German defence, Beckenbauer's skill in mid-field was plain to see, while Seeler, Held and

Haller were strikers of the highest class. They had the makings of a fine side; the odds against West Germany winning the Jules Rimet trophy dropped dramatically.

The soccer fans in the north-east corner of England lavished their affection on the North Koreans, inevitably dubbed the "diddy men." They soon showed that they were no novices, and were to provide one of the biggest shocks of the competition later on.

The Russians, ponderous in attack and uncompromising in their tackling, beat them 3—0. They could have got some more but for feeble finishing and wrapping their legs round the inexperienced Koreans.

England's two other opponents in Group One, France and Mexico, played a 1—1 draw in a game of missed chances. Mexico, thought to be one of the weakest teams ever to reach the final stages of a World Cup, had been beaten 8—0 on their last appearance at Wembley five years before.

This time they made full use of their tall and graceful centre-forward Borja, and by constantly interchanging positions threw the French off balance. Borja scored just after the interval, but France then began to take a grip on the game, and Hausser equalised with a twenty-yard shot.

On the same night Italy defeated Chile 2—0. In 1962 these two sides had met in a savage brawl, later to be known as the "Battle of Santiago". There was no fighting at Roker Park; the game was one long yawn. Having opened the scoring after ten minutes, the Italians spent the next eighty playing disinterested, walking football, until they got a second in the last minute.

Spain, the Champions of Europe, have promised so much and achieved so little in the World Cup that it was no surprise when they were beaten 2—1 by Argentina. They did not relish playing against a defence calculated to deter all but the most courageous. To begin with, the elegant Suarez took their crunching tackles with a shrug, but had had enough long before the end.

The Argentina centre-forward Artime scored twice, and Martinez replied for Spain. On the whole it was not an unpleasant game, and gave no inkling of the bother Argentina were to get themselves in later on.

When the draw for the grouping was made on 6th January, 1966 it looked certain that the fortunate spectators would be those who saw the Group Three matches at Liverpool and Manchester. Rather surprisingly, the Portugal—Hungary game at Old Trafford attracted fewer than 30,000 people.

Apart from the defeat of the weak Swiss team by West Germany, all the games so far had produced the anticipated defensive struggles. The Hungarians and Portuguese played a much more open game, with Portugal taking the lead in the second minute.

The goalkeeping in this match was slovenly; both 'keepers made bad errors, and were dropped for the next matches. Portugal ran out fairly easy winners by 3—1, but both sides had won a reputation for playing really attractive soccer — something that was clearly not the aim of the majority of teams.

With all sixteen having played one game, no outstanding team had emerged. The odds against Portugal and West Germany reaching the Final shortened; Brazil retained their place as favourites more on reputation than performance. Twenty-four hours later their hopes of winning their third World Cup had faded away. In the finest match of the competition so far they were beaten by the brilliant but unpredictable Hungarian side at Goodison Park.

Brazil were without Pele. He had received one knock too many in the previous game. Their attack lacked fire — and, mistakenly, they persisted in playing the veterans Djalma Santos and Bellini.

They were soon a goal down — and what a magnificent goal it was! Bene took a pass from Meszoly, beat Altair first on the outside and then on the inside, left Bellini stranded, and sent in a left foot shot between goalkeeper Gylmar and the post.

Tostao (*extreme right*) scores for Brazil against Hungary

Brazil fought back, and equalised a quarter of an hour later. Once again a free kick led to it. Garrincha and Lima got into position, but it was Lima who took the kick, surprising the wall of defenders. They had expected one of Garrincha's swerving thunderbolts. The ball rebounded to Tostao, who hit it past Gelei in the Hungarian goal.

But Brazil never looked like world champions, and in the second half the Hungarians got right on top. First Farkas scored with a beautifully-timed volley from Bene's centre, and Meszoly added a third from a penalty.

The Liverpool crowd were delighted with the display of both teams. They cheered them off the field at the end, reserving their loudest cheers for Florian Albert, the Hungarian centre-forward, who had given a magnificent display. Picking up the ball in mid-field and avoiding tackles with graceful ease, he showed how imaginative soccer can still be played no matter how many men stand guard in the penalty area. On this performance he looked one of the world's greatest footballers; only in the matter of finishing could Albert be faulted.

In contrast to the brilliant play at Goodison Park most of the games in the other groups were dull and pedestrian. North Korea and Chile played a 1–1 draw, and Uruguay and Spain had odd-goal victories over France and Switzerland respectively.

Russia were the first country to make certain of a place in the Quarter-finals by a 1–0 win over the disappointing Italians, while Portugal had little difficulty in defeating Bulgaria.

A bitter battle at Villa Park between West Germany and Argentina ended in a goalless draw. There was a great deal of chopping down and kicking opponents, and finally one of the Argentinian players was sent off.

England's next opponents were Mexico, who, like Uruguay, grouped their players in a negative formation, determined at all costs to stop their opponents from scoring.

The result was another unattractive match for the huge Wembley crowd and the millions watching on televison. There was one memorable moment. Bobby Charlton scored a spectacular goal in the thirty-seventh minute.

He collected the ball near the centre circle, ran on twenty yards, veered to the right, and then spun round to crash in a terrific shot.

With England one up at half-time and the Mexicans seemingly incapable of producing a worthwhile shot at goal, the crowd expected to see their side run up a good score. They were disappointed; there was just one more goal. Greaves took a perfect pass from Charlton, shot hard, and the Mexican 'keeper could only push the ball straight to the feet of Hunt, who promptly swept it into the net.

11

A clear victory, but one that did not inspire confidence. What changes would Alf Ramsey make for the next game? He had brought in Terry Paine instead of John Connelly, and Martin Peters instead of the injured Alan Ball. Obviously the defence would not be altered — Gordon Banks, George Cohen, Ray Wilson, Nobby Stiles, Jack Charlton and skipper Bobby Moore had done all that could be asked of them. But up in front only Bobby Charlton looked entirely convincing; for the rest it could be any four from ten.

Meanwhile Brazil shuffled their side like a pack of cards. They dropped Garrincha, Djalma Santos, Altair and many other former stars for the game against Portugal, which they had to win to stay in the competition. Seven of the team were making their first appearance in the series, but Pele was fit again, and so long as he was there they could not be taken lightly.

Unluckily for the champions he was injured again in the first half, following a collision, though by that time Brazil's cause was almost lost. Simoes had given Portugal the lead with a header and Eusebio made it two with another.

Pele returned limping, but could no longer make his presence felt. Although Rildo got one back for Brazil with a twenty-five yard shot, the irrepressible Eusebio made the game safe for Portugal.

Then came the biggest World Cup shock since England lost 1—0 to the United States of America in 1950. Italy, one of the favourites to win the trophy before the final stages began, lost to the North Koreans, and were out.

And when Russia beat Chile it meant that the North Koreans were in the last eight. Few people outside North Korea itself ever thought that would happen.

England were now bound to qualify unless they lost decisively to France. In view of the French record of one point from two matches, that seemed unlikely. Peters kept

his place, but there was yet another change on the right wing — Ian Callaghan replacing Paine.

The England–France game was another disappointing affair. Not because of modern defensive tactics this time; the French persisted with an old fashioned offside trap, and Hunt and Greaves were caught in it time after time. But, as often happens, it proved their undoing in the end.

Jackie Charlton had several defenders between himself and the goal when he moved through to head a Greaves cross. The ball struck a post, rebounded across the face of the goal and Hunt ran it over the line.

France needed at least a two-goal victory to stay in, and this was now clearly beyond them. They relaxed, and with the tension gone, began to play attacking football. For the first time in the series Banks had some hard work to do.

England's defence was well-drilled and resolute — perhaps too much so in the case of Stiles, who up-ended one or two Frenchmen without ceremony. It was while one of his victims was writhing on the ground that Hunt headed in a centre from Callaghan for England's second goal.

The Peruvian referee, apparently used to players in his own country play-acting, had refused to halt the game, but in this case the French player was genuinely injured.

England were lucky that the referee had not seen the actual incident. If he had, they would have had a free kick given against them, and Stiles may even have got his marching orders for a most reckless tackle. The goal counted; that's the luck of the game.

England thus finished at the top of Group One, followed by Uruguay. Nine goals were scored in the six games, none of which could be called anything but moderate.

West Germany headed Group Two, with Argentina second. Here the total of goals reached sixteen, of which Switzerland conceded nine. As in London, the football at Villa Park and Hillsborough had little sparkle about it. The crowds admired the competence and organization of the Germans, and occasional flashes of brilliance from the Spanish — and that was about all.

Group Three showed an entirely different picture. Portugal, Hungary and Brazil thrilled Merseyside with their scintillating play. Even Bulgaria raised their standard to such an extent that sometimes they were nearly as good as their opponents. Twenty-one goals were scored, and it was a pity that only two teams could go forward. They were Portugal, the most improved European team, with maximum points, and Hungary, who, if the Cup had been awarded for entertainment, would have walked away with it at that stage.

Group Four in the north-east was poorly supported. With the failure of Italy, there was little glamour about the players. The Russians got exactly half the total of twelve goals scored, but, apart from veteran goalkeeper Lev Yashin, they were not a very attractive side to watch. The very fact of North Korea qualifying emphasised the standard of play.

And so to the Quarter-finals.

Would they produce four thrilling games? It would need a miracle. Three? Most unlikely. Two? Possibly. One? The best bet, but which one would it be?

It turned out to be a black day for the two South American teams. Uruguay had two players sent off; Argentina, one.

It was a black day for the imaginative and talented Hungarians, too. They went down 2–1 to a Russian side abundantly equipped with muscle and speed. They were a goal behind after five minutes, and never really got going.

West Germany held a one-goal lead at the interval against Uruguay, and the match could have gone either way. But early in the second half the Uruguayan captain, Troche, and centre-forward Silva were both sent off after some vicious tackling. The Germans, not as blameless as they tried to appear in the two incidents, then scored more or less as they pleased.

The spectators at Wembley had a choice. They could watch what was happening on the field, which, to begin with at any rate, was a sheer waste of time, or they could

Eusebio scores Portugal's second goal against North Korea from a penalty.

look up at the scoreboard and see what was going on in the clash between Portugal and North Korea. In the first minute Pak Seung Zin had put North Korea one up. At Wembley there was a gasp.

Within half an hour the scoreboard read "North Korea 3, Portugal 0." The Wembley spectators could hardly believe their eyes, but soon afterwards they were forced to take notice of the sensational incidents that were taking place in the game they had come to watch.

From the kick-off the imperious West German referee had blown his whistle at every opportunity. There was no lack of physical contact, so free kicks were two a penny. Then the fouling really built up, the notebook came out, and someone suggested that the official would soon have enough numbers in it to start a bingo session.

Rattin, the Argentina captain and a habi-tual offender, was then seen to be pursuing the referee round the field, pointing to his armband, and shouting. He was promptly ordered off the field.

That did it!

At first Rattin refused to go. Then he went slowly towards the touchline where the Argentinian officials were waiting, followed by the rest of the team.

Then followed eight minutes of argument, with the referee adamant that the game must go on without Rattin. At one time it seemed that it would be abandoned, but at last the South Americans agreed to restart.

Meanwhile the half-time score showed that Portugal had scored twice, and were now only a goal in arrears.

Ten men always face an uphill task, and in this game extra time could be played if the scores were level at the end of ninety minutes. Argentina's only real chance was

Geoff Hurst heads the vital goal for England against Argentina.

to deny England a goal, and hope to go through at the end by the spin of a coin.

They could not quite manage it.

Twelve minutes from time Peters took a pass from Wilson, and sent over a fine cross. Geoff Hurst (who had replaced the injured Greaves) had cleverly moved into position, and he glanced the ball finely with his head past the 'keeper and into the net.

And the scoreboard showed that Portugal had beaten North Korea by five goals to three. Four of their goals had come from Eusebio, including two penalties.

So it was Russia versus West Germany, and Portugal versus England for the Semi-finals.

Strong-arm tactics were well to the fore at Goodison Park, and the Russians got by far the worst of it. Within ten minutes their inside forward Sabo was a passenger, his left leg virtually useless.

Savage tackles followed one another in quick succession, both sides contributing equally to the roughness of the game. As half-time approached the Russian winger Chislenko was dispossessed by a heavy tackle and saw the ball swept out to Haller, who hammered it into the net.

A minute later Chislenko, in pain from the badly gashed knee he had suffered in the tackle and obviously incensed that his team was a goal behind instead of a free kick being awarded for the tackle on him, lashed out at the nearest German.

It happened to be Held, and it took place right in front of the referee. Held rolled about on the ground, and Chislenko was sent off.

That was the end of Russia's progress in the World Cup. Nine men and a passenger had no chance, in spite of the efforts of Voronin, a really great half back, and the coolness of goalkeeper Yashin.

Beckenbauer scored again for Germany mid-way through the second half, while Porkujan snatched a consolation goal for the Russians three minutes from time.

In the other Semi-final the football played by Portugal and England fascinated everyone who saw it. The two sides provided a contrast in styles, but both set out to score goals right from the kick-off. And England, with Alan Ball keeping his place, did that job just a little better.

Eusebio, Portugal's danger man, paid the price of fame. He could produce few of those thrilling runs he had shown in previous games because Stiles shadowed him intelligently and without recourse to chopping him down.

After a series of thrilling attacks by both sides, England got the vital first goal. Wilson sent a long through ball into the penalty area, where Hunt fastened on to it and kicked it against the advancing goalkeeper. Pereira could not hold it, and the ball bounced out to Bobby Charlton, who shot it calmly into the vacant net.

Ten minutes from the end Hurst took a pass from Cohen, rounded his opponent and pulled the ball back for Charlton to run on to. Bobby thumped it straight and true — and England were two up.

Portugal were not beaten yet. A centre from Simoes deceived Banks, and Torres headed the ball towards the open goal. Jackie Charlton could do no more than palm the ball away — an obvious penalty kick. Eusebio, as usual, made no mistake from the spot. 2--1. And England's hopes of reaching the Final without conceding a goal were dashed.

Portugal were voted by a lot of people to be the most talented of all the sixteen teams. As one spectator remarked, as he left Wembley that night, "If that had been the Final and Portugal had won, we should have had nothing to complain about. But now we've beaten them, I think we have the edge on West Germany in tactics and stamina, and there is nothing between us in skill." Perhaps he just about summed it all up.

Portugal had some consolation by winning the match for third place in the tournament when they beat Russia 2—1, and in

Eusebio they undoubtedly had the star attraction of the three weeks of soccer.

He scored nine goals (including four penalties) while his nearest rival — Haller of West Germany — could only manage five, and he gave pleasure to everyone who saw his skill with the ball and his sportsmanship.

England's display in winning the World Cup was a personal triumph for Alf Ramsey, their team manager, who had planned it for three years. Dedicated to the game and to his players and impervious to all criticism, he moulded eleven individuals into a team, decided its tactics and brought the side to its peak of fitness at just the right moment.

Ramsey was fortunate that he had no injuries to key players apart from Greaves. Jimmy was fit for the Final, and Ramsey had the awkward decision of whether or not to bring him in as one of the front line. He decided not to alter a team that had won its last two matches, and his judgement could not be faulted.

Against Portugal they had the look of greatness. Forgotten were the earlier mediocre performances against opponents whose only aim was to prevent them from scoring. And against West Germany, equally splendid opponents, they showed strength, courage and skill.

The players — all twenty two of them in the World Cup squad — responded magnificently to Ramsey's leadership. If any could be singled out for special praise they were Bobby Moore, a cool and inspiring captain, Bobby Charlton, elegant and effective in everything he did, and Gordon Banks, easily the best goalkeeper in the sixteen teams.

The whole defence inspired confidence. On the one occasion they faltered — in the Final — the hard-working forwards, Hurst, Hunt and Ball saved the day.

Without detracting in any way from England's great performance, it must be remembered that they had the advantage of playing in front of their own supporters. And, unlike some home international matches in which

Manager Alf Ramsey — the man behind England's triumph.

they have actually been booed, this support was tremendous at Wembley throughout the competition, but especially in the Semi-final and Final.

In the previous seven World Cups, the host country has won the trophy twice, been beaten finalists twice and taken third place once.

When West Germany won the trophy in 1954 the matches were played in nearby Switzerland, and they, too, had tremendous support. When Italy carried off the Cup for the second time in 1938 the tournament was held in France. No European country has yet succeeded in winning the Jules Rimet trophy when the final stages have taken place on the other side of the Atlantic.

So if England, now Champions of the World at soccer, retain it when the next World Cup competition is played in Mexico in 1970 they will have achieved something really outstanding.

The Winning Eight

Dennis Smith

Both Manchester clubs were elected to the Football League in 1891; United straight into the First Division, and City to the second.

Which of them has been longer in Division One since then?

Many people would say "Manchester United" because they have played in the top class for the past twenty years without a break, and are now one of the premier clubs in England.

They'd be wrong.

City have played forty-seven seasons in the First Division compared with United's forty-three. And they've made more Cup-final appearances too, although both clubs have won the trophy three times.

City's last spell in Division Two started in 1963, and by the middle of last season manager Joe Mercer had got together a fine combination of youth and experience. All he had to do was to blend it into a winning side.

Experience was contributed by that brilliant Irish international Johnny Crossan, an inspiring skipper; promising winger Mike Summerbee came to Maine Road from Swindon Town, and the much sought-after Colin Bell from Bury; local boy Neil Young soon got among the goals.

A resolute defence, in which Bobby Kennedy and George Heslop were outstanding, played a great part in the team's success.

Although Manchester City were always among the pacemakers in the Second Division, the struggle for promotion was not settled until the last few games. They were pushed all the way by Huddersfield Town, Coventry City, Southampton, Wolves and Bristol City, but in the end they finished Champions of Division Two for the sixth time in their history.

Huddersfield's hopes of joining them crashed when they were beaten 2—0 at home by Coventry in their last match, and this left Southampton in the position of having to get only one point from two games to become a First Division side for the first time in their history.

They came to Brisbane Road to meet the bottom club, Leyton Orient, already doomed to relegation.

The Saints were so nervous that their forwards could hardly string two passes together in the first half, and they were a goal down in the first few minutes. From a breakaway in the second half Terry Paine got the all-important equaliser with a header.

In their last match they played a goalless draw at Maine Road against Manchester City to finish runners-up.

Southampton, founded in 1885, were members of the Southern League until 1920, when they joined the newly-formed Third Division of the Football League. They won promotion in 1922 and stayed in Division Two for twenty-four consecutive seasons, twice coming near to First Division status but narrowly failing each time.

In 1948—9 they were eight points clear of their nearest challengers at one time. Promotion seemed certain, but they fell away and failed by one point.

Next year they got even closer. After a

''Come on, then. Try and take it off me,'' invites Johnny Crossan, Manchester City's Irish international skipper.

close struggle with the two Sheffield clubs all three finished with the same number of points. But Sheffield Wednesday had the best goal average, and once again the Saints had to remain behind.

Then came reaction, and they went back to the Third Division three years later.

Returning to the Second in 1960, they have challenged the leaders year after year, and were considered by many to be the best team outside the First Division. As well as Paine, John Sydenham on the other wing has consistently penetrated the most obdurate defences.

Martin Chivers, England Under-23 international, has been their leading marksman, while the twinkling feet of Jimmy Melia, former England international, provided the necessary guile to create the openings.

Last season Southampton strengthened their defence. They bought Campbell Forsyth from Kilmarnock to keep goal, Tony Knapp was in fine form at centre-half, while a shrewd move on the part of manager Ted Bates secured full-back David Webb from Leyton Orient just at the right moment in the race for the top.

Teams that have made the First Division for the first time in their history in the last decade have not stayed there very long. Leyton Orient and Northampton Town each lasted only one season; Ipswich Town were there for three, but managed to pull off the League Championship in the first of them.

Southampton may not be able to equal Ipswich's feat, but they seem to have a better chance of a longer run in the top class, since they can attract the support of a much

Southampton FC 1965–6. *Back row, left to right:* Huxford, Chivers, Webb, Hollywood, Walker, White, Forsyth. *Front row, left to right:* Sydenham, Paine, Knapp, Melia, Dean, Williams.

larger town than either Northampton or Ipswich.

It is interesting to note that Southampton are the first club south of London itself to play First Division football since Portsmouth were relegated in 1959.

In contrast to the protracted struggle in the Second Division it was obvious long before the end of the season that the two teams to go up from Division Three would be Hull City and Millwall.

At one time Hull were regular members of Division Two, but they were last there ten years ago. Since then, chairman Harold Needler has poured vast sums of money into the club, and in Cliff Britton, the former Everton and England half-back, he has got one of the shrewdest brains in soccer as manager.

In 1965 Britton bought three costly forwards – Ian Butler and Ken Houghton from Rotherham, and Ken Wagstaff from Mansfield Town. They are known as the "Glamour Boys" at Boothferry Park, and between them they scored the majority of Hull's goals last season. Local find Chris Chilton was also a regular scorer, while both wing-halves, Jarvis and Simpkin, quickly responded to Britton's flair for the game.

As well as winning promotion Hull City had a fine Cup run, reaching the Sixth Round and including Nottingham Forest and Southampton among their victims.

Then they came to Stamford Bridge and played a 2–2 draw with Chelsea before going out to the London club in the replay in front of a crowd of more than 45,000.

Hull City could certainly increase the Yorkshire representation in the First Division before very long. The support is there – and so is the talent.

For Millwall it is their third spell in the Second Division. They were last there in 1948, and spent four seasons in the Fourth Division from 1958 to 1962. Their best effort in the FA Cup in recent times was in 1957, when they reached the Fifth Round before being beaten 4–1 at home by Birmingham, but they have done much better than that in the past, reaching the Semi-finals three times.

For their fine defensive record Millwall owed a lot to their England Under-23 goalkeeper, Alex Stepney. Formerly with ama-

Alex Stepney.

teurs Tooting and Mitcham, this fine young 'keeper is strongly fancied for full international honours very soon.

Alex is now a Chelsea player, having been transferred by Millwall last May for £50,000 — a record fee for a goalkeeper in Britain.

An effective forward line included Len Julians, who returned to Millwall after a period with Arsenal and Nottingham Forest, and is now their coach, Chris Clarke, Mike Brown and Eamonn Dunphy, previously with York City.

And for the second season in succession the Lions were undefeated at home.

Some people think that four teams should be promoted and relegated from *all* Divisions instead of just the lowest.

Certainly this greater opportunity provided an exciting struggle in Division Four last year, involving no fewer than six teams — Doncaster Rovers, Darlington, Torquay United, Colchester United, Tranmere Rovers and Luton Town. A seventh, Chester, were close behind.

A week before the season ended it was still impossible to say which four of these six would eventually go up.

Doncaster Rovers were the first to make certain. They were first elected to Division Two of the Football League in 1901, but two years later failed to get re-elected although two clubs finished lower than they did. They got back in 1904, but had a disastrous time and won only three League games out of thirty-four. This time they did finish bottom, and failed in their bid for re-election. They returned to League football when the Third Division (North) was extended to twenty-two clubs in 1923.

Since then they have had three spells of Second Division soccer, and it would not be surprising to see them back there again before long.

The second club to make sure of Third Division soccer this year was Darlington, whose story is told later in this book.

Luton's rather surprising failure at Newport in their last game but one was received with great relief at Plainmoor, as it meant the end of Torquay's anxious wait. They were back in Division Three after an absence of four years.

The last place was then virtually between Colchester and Luton.

Tranmere still had a slight chance because if they both lost and Colchester were beaten by something like a six-goal margin they would be promoted. But it was a faint hope indeed — and a bitter disappointment to a side that had headed the table for much of the season.

Both Colchester and Luton had only been relegated the year before, and were desperately anxious to return to Third Division soccer.

Colchester, away to Newport and having a superior goal average, needed only to draw to make sure of going up. Luton had to go to Chester to play a re-arranged game, the first one having been abandoned because of a cloudburst when the Hatters were two goals in the lead.

Colchester did not succeed at Newport, losing 2–1; Luton drew 1–1 at Chester. So Colchester went up on goal average with the help of the deluge that had descended on their unlucky rivals a few weeks before. And Luton Town had to wait for another season to begin their climb back to a higher class.

It seems incredible that the Cup-finalists of 1959, then a successful First Division club, should now be lingering in Division Four, but once the slide begins it takes a lot of stopping.

Clubs currently playing Fourth Division soccer that have at one time or another played in the First Division include Bradford, Bradford City, Brentford and Notts County (as well as Luton), while Barnsley and Bradford City have won the F.A. Cup.

The road back in soccer is certainly a tough one.

Spotlight on Bobby Moore

The playing record of Bobby Moore is re-markable. At the age of twenty-five he has already played for England in two World Cup series, and has led West Ham United to victory in the FA Cup and the European Cup-winners' Cup. Only a player dedicated to soccer could have achieved such fame while so young.

As soon as he was old enough Bobby joined the ground staff at Upton Park. He

made eighteen appearances for England's youth team (a record), and made his League debut for West Ham when he was only seventeen. In 1960 his intelligent ball distri-bution, fearless tackling and tireless energy earned him a regular place in the side, and in the same season he became captain of the England Under-23 team.

He showed obvious powers of leadership, and set a fine example to the other players by his sportsmanship and intelligent play. West Ham were quick to recognise this, and they made him skipper of the side. Bobby's shrewdness and his ability to sum up a game and take the necessary steps to counter the tactical moves of the opposition have made him one of the outstanding footballers in soccer to-day.

He played his first game for England in a full international in Peru in 1962, and has been an automatic choice for one of the half back positions ever since. When Jimmy Armfield dropped out of the side in 1964 the choice of his successor as captain of England gave the selectors no problem. Bobby Moore had shown them that he was the obvious man for the job by the manner in which he had skippered West Ham and the England Under-23 side.

In the same year Bobby was elected Foot-baller of the Year by the Football Writers' Association, and he responded to this honour by leading West Ham to victory in the FA Cup. In one of the best Finals ever seen at Wembley the London club beat Preston North End 3–2. The following year he had another Wembley triumph, when

England half backs, Bobby Moore and Jackie Charlton in a duel for the ball in the game between West Ham and Leeds United.

West Ham won the European Cup-winners' Cup.

You have to have some luck to succeed as well as Moore has, and Bobby is the first to admit that things have gone pretty well for him ever since he started playing football for a living. But there's more to it than luck.

In an article for *The Boys' Book of Soccer for 1964* Bobby Moore said this:—

'I've lots to learn about soccer, but I'm determined that I'm going to learn more and more about the game. I'm going to keep myself in tip-top condition, and keep practising as hard as I can. Then, when 1966 comes along and Pele and Co. come here to try and win the World Cup for the third time in succession, I hope I'm good enough to be picked for a team that's going to do their best to prevent them from doing it.'

He certainly was, when the England team came on to the field at Wembley against Uruguay in the opening game, it was Bobby Moore who led them out.

Heavy Going

When the players of Benfica or Real Madrid give a superb display of soccer on a hard, true pitch some people say "They couldn't do it on the heavy grounds that we have in England in mid-winter."

That's a half truth.

Clubs used to playing on hard grounds have beaten many of our League sides on wet pitches. Even thick, sticky mud can't completely nullify skilful ball play.

The play-off match between Leeds United and the Spanish club, Real Zaragoza, took place on a quagmire. The Spaniards put up such a brilliant exhibition to win 3—1 that the sporting Elland Road crowd cheered them off the field at the end, disappointed as they were at their own side losing.

But conditions like those do make the task of trying to play top-class soccer very much harder. Waterlogged pitches were to some extent responsible for the kick and rush soccer that until recently some of our League teams found so successful. With defenders sliding about all over the place, the tearaway forwards had an obvious advantage. Long kicks up the field and long passes out to the

Leeds United *versus* Real Zaragoza in the Inter-Cities Fairs Cup. Yarza, the Spanish goalkeeper, resists a challenge from Jim Storrie.

Muddy conditions at White Hart Lane. Alan Gilzean (Spurs) and Northampton goalkeeper Brian Harvey in a struggle for the ball with Northampton right half John Kurila (No. 4) on hand.

wings — inaccurate as many of them were — often led to goals. The evolution of tactics like the four man defensive line made things more and more difficult for attackers — even in slippery conditions.

Mud is a great leveller, it is said. How exciting it can be when, in a mud bath in February in which players can barely distinguish one of their own side from an opponent unless he shouts, a little club knocks a big one out of the FA Cup.

Perhaps it is. But it is not often done by skilful soccer. It is more likely that the pitch is quite unsuitable for playing football on at all, and accurate passing is out of the question.

What can be done about it?

We can't stop it raining. We can't postpone matches simply because the ground is half waterlogged, although referees today seem to be more strict about when a pitch is playable than they used to be.

We could play our football in the summer. Not that it doesn't rain in Britain in the summer — sometimes it is wetter than the winter. But at least the ground dries up more quickly, and nearly all the matches would be played on firm pitches.

It would be better for spectators, too. It might even halt the continuing decline in attendances.

Many experts firmly believe that top-class soccer should not be played at all during the months of December, January and February. They think the season should be in two halves — from August to November, and from March to June.

But if we must play our soccer in the winter, what can be done to stop pitches churning up into a mass of mud a few minutes after the games start?

25

Well, we can see that the ground is adequately drained. That sounds obvious, but many pitches still aren't. The drainage system may have been installed many years before, when knowledge of the best type of drainage of any particular type of soil was much less than it is now.

Much can be done to ensure a good growth of grass. The problem here is that at present the close season for football is so short (and getting shorter each year) that the grass does not have time to get properly rooted.

Thick velvety turf such as that on the Wembley pitch enables the players to have a fine surface on which to work. But it seems that they are not used to it on their own grounds to judge by the number of serious leg injuries that have occurred in matches there.

Of course Wembley does not have anything like the number of matches played on it that League grounds do.

What else can be done?

Most clubs cover the goal areas with plastic covers during wet weather, and these remain comparatively dry. But it is no simple matter to cover a larger area with plastic covers, and in any case these have to be removed well before the start of a game, and a few hours' rain can create plenty of mud.

Perhaps the best hope of providing a solution to the problem of heavy grounds lies in the drying of the soil by heat. Some clubs already have underpitch electric heating which prevents the ground from freezing and melts snow lying on the surface.

It is ideal for keeping the ground open for drainage during icy weather; unfortunately it does not manage to keep the soil drier in very wet weather.

Frequent mud baths for footballers therefore seem inevitable if we continue to have our soccer season in mid-winter. If we are to play the majority of our games on grounds that are heavy, can we really expect our players to be at their best when they have to play on bone-hard pitches in sunnier countries?

In the December gloom Alan Mullery scrambles the ball away during the game against Chelsea.

Everton Fight Back

The Merseysiders came to Wembley with an unique record. Not a single goal had been scored against them on the way to the Final. Within five minutes they were a goal down.

Their opponents, Sheffield Wednesday, arrived the hard way. Not a single home game. Yet they had won each of their earlier matches at the first attempt. And for the greater part of the ninety minutes it seemed that they would leave London with their record intact.

The 1966 Cup Final was contested by two sides that had not played at Wembley for more than thirty years. Sheffield Wednesday's last appearance there was in 1935, when they beat West Bromwich Albion 4—2; Everton's, two years before, when they defeated Manchester City 3—0.

All last season football enthusiasts had been talking about a Manchester United versus Chelsea Final, but these two glamour teams fell at the last hurdle — the Semi-finals. When it failed to materialise some people (not those in Liverpool and Sheffield, of course) dismissed the Final tie as a dismal climax to the season and likely to provide second-class entertainment.

Well, they were wrong.

It turned out to be one of the most enjoyable Finals that Wembley has seen for a long time, with both teams rising above the mediocrity of their League positions to play positive, open football.

Everton were slight favourites, although on the morning of the match some newspapers tipped Wednesday to win despite the absence of Vic Mobley, their centre-half.

Their loss was balanced, on paper at any rate, by the absence, also through injury, of Everton's international centre-forward, Fred Pickering.

An early goal is just the thing to settle Wembley nerves, and in the fifth minute the Wednesday right half, Peter Eustace, took a throw-in on the left. He threw the ball to David Ford, who squared it into the middle.

It was met by Jim McCalliog, the centre forward, and he put in a left foot shot of no great pace about fifteen yards from goal.

Gordon West appeared to have got it covered, but as he moved to one side to meet it the ball deflected off his full back, Ray Wilson, swung across to the other side, and left him helpless.

A soft goal, but it put the Wednesday youngsters in the lead.

They were perhaps a trifle fortunate to keep it. Not long afterwards Ron Springett dived and swept Alex Young's feet from under him just as he was about to shoot well inside the box. Everton's claims for a penalty looked justified, but the referee waved play on.

Referees don't like giving penalty kicks in Cup Finals if they can possibly avoid it.

For the rest of the first half it was cut and thrust. Both sides had their chances, but the Wednesday youngsters were coping ably with the big occasion, and their forwards looked the more dangerous in midfield.

Ten minutes after the interval, however, the game suddenly changed from a tactical battle to a thrilling spectacle that had the huge crowd roaring with excitement.

Two ways of looking at Sheffield Wednesday's first goal. *Above:* Gordon West sprawls on the ground after failing to stop Jim McCalliog's shot. *Below:* McCalliog (side-faced in centre of picture, white shirt) turns in triumph to meet the hugs of his team-mates.

Johnny Fantham, who, with Springett, Eustace and Gerry Young, had been Sheffield's inspiration, forged past two defenders and fired in a tremendous drive that West could not hold.

The ball bounced back out of his arms, and Ford raced up to slide it into the net for Wednesday's second goal.

This should have sealed the Yorkshire club's victory. It is rare indeed for a team with

Above: John Quinn of Sheffield Wednesday tackled by Colin Harvey of Everton. *Below:* Ron Springett well beaten by Mike Trebilcock's equaliser.

a two goal lead and eleven fit players to lose a Cup Final. Unfortunately for the Wednesday they did not hold that lead long enough to consolidate it.

A header from Derek Temple on the edge of the penalty area looked harmless enough, but the covering in the Wednesday middle was found wanting for almost the first time. Everton's striking inside forward, Mike Trebilcock, found himself all alone, and he was able to take careful aim with his right foot and put the ball past Springett.

Five minutes later he scored again. Alex Scott lobbed a free kick into the goalmouth, Young headed the ball back intelligently to Trebilcock, and the young inside forward hit it first time to send it swerving inside the unsighted goalkeeper's right hand post.

The scores were level.

At this juncture a few of the Everton supporters could contain themselves no longer. They rushed on to the field to mob their heroes, and the Law dashed after them.

One fan, chased half the length of the field by a policeman, had the presence of mind to take off his coat just as the policeman grabbed it, and down went the cop, much to the merriment of the spectators. One of his colleagues took up the chase, and finally got his man.

When the game was resumed a subtle difference appeared in the play of Sheffield Wednesday. All the fight seemed to have gone out of them. Their defence, so strikingly sound in the earlier minutes of the game, now looked tottery. Their forwards no longer found one another with their first-half confidence.

A spirited chase following Everton's second goal. A Merseyside fan evades capture by slipping off his coat, and the genial policeman enters into the fun of the thing by falling over.

The victorious Everton team do a lap of honour with the Cup after their victory.

And in the seventy-third minute came the deciding goal.

Gerry Young had ample time and space to collect a loose ball in midfield, but he appeared to take his eye off it, and it rolled away off his boot. Before he could recover Temple had gathered the ball and was sprinting for goal with only the goalkeeper to beat.

It was in these vital seconds that Temple's coolness and experience were to prove decisive. Goalkeepers like Springett know all there is to know about a situation like this; how far and just when to advance and narrow the angle so as to give the advancing forward the smallest area of target to aim at.

Temple showed his class. He steered the ball some thirty yards upfield, veered slightly to his right and then crashed the ball low and true into the net past the advancing Springett.

Sheffield Wednesday were still not quite finished, but their touch had gone and with

it their luck. Once a flick from Fantham's heel curled just over the crossbar, but as the minutes ticked by the now-confident Everton played as if they never had any doubt about the ultimate result.

So the Cup, as well as the League Championship, came to the city of Liverpool. Ten years before Manchester had achieved a similar monopoly, with United winning the League and City the Cup.

But in those days European club football was in its infancy. Today, to play in one of the European competitions is the main ambition of every First Division club, and it sometimes appears that domestic matches are simply a means to that end. But you still can't get a ticket for the Cup Final without a lot of difficulty, all the same.

Everton brought the Cup to Goodison Park for the third time in their history. Thanks to their great second half fight back they just about deserved to do so.

31

Peter Thompson — Liverpool and England.

It's Great at the Top

Peter Thompson

I admire my footballing friends who play their hearts out every week for teams struggling against relegation in front of mediocre support.

I admire them — but I don't envy them.

Who wouldn't rather be a member of a winning side — a team in the race for either the League title or the FA Cup, and taking part in one of the big European club competitions every year?

Let's face it. Success is a pleasant thing. Everyone enjoys it. If it comes your way you don't have to get swollen-headed about it, of course. Very few players do. They know that any individual, however talented he may be, can claim but a small share in a club's success.

I couldn't have been luckier in my career since the day I joined Liverpool. In my first season we won the League Championship, the next the FA Cup and last year the League title again. Every year we've taken part in either the European Cup or the European Cup-winners' Cup.

It has been a great privilege for me to go on the field every week with this great bunch of sportsmen, and to learn more and more about the game from such a dedicated and experienced manager as Mr. Shankly.

When I first came to Anfield from Preston North End in 1963 I had to contend with a certain amount of banter from both players and spectators. They hadn't forgotten what happened in the Preston-Liverpool Fifth Round cup-tie two seasons before.

The two clubs had fought two goalless draws, and had to meet for a third time in Manchester. I got the only goal of the match for Preston to knock Liverpool out of the Cup. I think they've really forgiven me, but even now that goal is mentioned in the course of conversation and someone gives me a reproachful look.

I was born and brought up in Carlisle — rather a long way from any main centre of professional soccer. I was very keen on the game from childhood, and although I went along to Brunton Park occasionally to see Carlisle United I much preferred playing to watching.

I was picked for Cumberland schoolboys and later for England schoolboys, and when I left school I joined Preston North End as an apprentice.

At that time I was an inside forward, and it was in that position that I took part in the Schoolboys' International against Scotland in 1958. Our side included Terry Venables, now with Tottenham Hotspur, Bert Murray, of Chelsea, and Ron Boyce, now with West Ham.

We won 3–1, and one of my not-so-pleasant memories of the match was up-ending Billy Bremner and giving away a penalty. The Scots missed it, but Billy reminds me of the incident when we play Leeds United.

Preston were then in the First Division, and Tom Finney was still thrilling the crowds all over the country with his ball-play even though he had reached the veteran stage. Tom retired in 1960, and everyone knew that his inspiration was going to be sadly missed at Deepdale.

33

I made my League debut the following year as a centre-forward. I made very little impression there, and later moved to the left wing. Our attack simply could not score goals, and we began slipping down the table.

A late rally failed to save us from relegation, and my first season in League football was a pretty unhappy experience. I had soon learned the meaning of failure.

Looking back, it may have been a blessing in disguise so far as I was concerned. I don't think I was really ready for First Division soccer. Some of the games in the lower class the following season with their greater emphasis on physical contact and smaller demands on skill helped to toughen me up and give me experience of all types of play.

Preston have the reputation of playing football that is pretty to watch, but sometimes lacks bite. That was a fault that had to be remedied by the youngsters in the side. Soon the goals began to come, and a good Cup run gave us confidence.

I have already mentioned that I got the goal that knocked Liverpool out of the Cup that year. In the previous Round something happened that still makes me laugh when I think of it.

We were playing Weymouth at Deepdale, and just before the kick-off thick fog came down. The game began, but within a short time it became so dense that we couldn't see the ball or distinguish opponents from our own side.

The referee blew his whistle indicating suspension of play, but several players didn't hear it and wandered aimlessly about in the gloom.

At last both teams got together in the boiler room to await the inevitable decision to abandon the game. I looked across at the Weymouth side, and noticed their goalkeeper wasn't there.

A search party went out, and found him still guarding his goal.

He didn't even know that the game had been stopped ten minutes' before!

Manchester United put us out in the Sixth Round, but only by 2–1 after a goalless draw at Deepdale.

In my three seasons of League soccer with Preston goals seemed hard to come by; at Liverpool I found myself in a side that apparently encountered little difficulty. Roger Hunt and Ian St John seemed to find the net in almost every game.

The 1963–4 Championship race was a see-saw struggle between Manchester United, Everton, Tottenham Hotspur and ourselves. We put in a grandstand finish, collecting six points from our three games at Easter and taking over the leadership.

We clinched the title with a 5–0 win over Arsenal at Anfield. I got a couple that afternoon, and brought my total for the season to six.

Only another twenty-five and I would have equalled Roger Hunt's aggregate. Well, we can't all score them, and at Liverpool nobody cares whose names appear on the score-sheet so long as the team keeps on winning.

Next season saw us carry off the FA Cup for the first time in the club's history, beating Leeds United 2–1 in the Final. It wasn't a great game; Leeds are always a difficult side to beat, and we only managed it in extra time.

A much more exciting affair was our struggle with Inter-Milan in the semi-finals of the European Cup.

We won the first leg at home 3–1, and had high hopes of being the first British club to reach the final of Europe's premier competition.

But we made a disastrous start in the return game in Italy, and found ourselves two goals down in ten minutes. We lost 4–3 on aggregate, but our experience was turned to good account when, as Cup-winners, we played in the European Cup-winners' Cup the following year.

Peter evades a sliding tackle by Fulham's Barrett at Craven Cottage last season. This was a game that Liverpool didn't win; a 2—0 victory meant two precious points for the London club.

Last season we went to the top of the League table in November — and stayed there to the end. In fact from February onwards it was really only a question of who would be runners-up to us. We had a lead of eight points over our nearest rivals. Several clubs had games in hand, but I know from experience that these are not the advantage that they appear to be. I'd much rather have points in the bag.

With the rosy prospect of another League Championship victory (Liverpool's seventh by the way, equalling Arsenal's record)

entitling us to a place in this season's European Cup, we could concentrate our efforts in trying to emulate Spurs and West Ham and win the Cup-winners' Cup.

We reached the Final, removing among others the Hungarian side, Honved, and Glasgow Celtic on the way, and earned the right to meet the strong German team, Borussia Dortmund.

The game was played at Hampden Park so our supporters did not have very far to travel, but unfortunately they did not have a lot to cheer about that evening.

I think we had slightly the better of a goalless first half, but a quarter of an hour after the interval the Germans went ahead with a fine goal from their centre-forward, Held.

Not long afterwards I got away on the right wing, centred from the by-line and Roger Hunt hit home a terrific shot for the equaliser.

The scores were level at the end of ninety minutes and after the first period of extra time. Then Borussia Dortmund got the winner — and what a lucky goal it was.

Held got clean through, but Tom Lawrence came out of his goal and dived at his feet to make a splendid save on the edge of the penalty area.

The ball rebounded to the right wing, where it went straight to the outside right, Libuda.

He took careful aim, and from long range sent in a slow, dropping shot to the far corner of the unguarded goal.

We all held our breath as Ron Yeats made a desperate effort to prevent the ball from going into the net, but as he dived the ball struck the inside of the post and went in.

Disappointment? Yes, but that's all part of the game.

Last season is forgotten; this year we plan to be the first British team to win the European Cup—the top club trophy in the world.

Roger Hunt equalises for Liverpool in the Cup-winners' Cup, but Borussia Dortmund get the winner in extra time.

Crystalmas Crackers

Cyril Hughes

The future of football is a topic of continuous discussion at national and international levels.

I have therefore consulted a highly unreliable crystal ball, supplemented by dozens of those paper 'fortune' slips that the manufacturers put inside Christmas crackers in the hope that you won't notice what rubbish the toys are.

Together, these well-tried sources indicate certain trends for the remainder of the current season which all those interested in the game will ignore at their peril.

Indications for January are bleak. The crystal glows white, which may mean unseasonable heat, or may mean the opposite. Many players have difficulty in keeping their feet on the ground. Several clubs subsequently have difficulty in keeping their heads above water.

The Pools firms announce that they have sufficient imaginary results of imaginary matches to keep the coupons going for the rest of the season.

The 580th Football League club manager to do so since the war parts company with his club. He says: 'I haven't actually been sacked – they just won't let me in the ground any more.' He refuses an offer of employment as a car salesman on the grounds that the job lacks security.

A famous First Division star asks for a transfer because his club insists on paying him more than he thinks he is worth.

A well-known sports writer is expelled from the National Union of Journalists because he reports a Liverpool home match without using the phrase 'the white-hot furnace of Spion Kop.'

As the month changes, the crystal glows white again, which may mean . . . weatherwise, February is just January plus pancakes, though there are indications that it may be a slightly shorter month.

Several clubs announce their intention of 'concentrating on the League' for the rest of the season. By a coincidence, all the teams concerned have recently been knocked out of the FA Cup.

Marshmallow Wanderers FC announce their intention of concentrating on obtaining membership of a League of any kind, and invite proposals from organizations of sufficiently low standard.

A famous international star demands a transfer because his club manager insists on playing him in the first team when he believes that his current form is better suited to the reserves.

A newspaper prints, for the 150th time this season, the headline: 'This England Team Will Not Do'. Mr Alf. Ramsey, the England team manager, sends a note of congratulation to the editor.

Of the fifteen players hailed by the Press as 'boy wonders' at the beginning of the season, two are still to be found actually playing in their clubs' first elevens.

The 600th Football League club manager to do so since the war parts company with his club. He says: 'I haven't actually been sacked – but feel I no longer have the full confidence of the Board since they threw me down the stairs.' To mark the occasion, the

Football League Management Committee present the ex-manager with a suitably inscribed travelling bag.

A well-known sports writer is demoted to the women's page of his paper because he reports an Everton home match without using the phrase 'the seething cauldron of Goodison Park.'

A Third Division club makes two records in one day by appointing its twentieth manager in three years and its first director ever with a practical knowledge of football.

ABC Rangers press on with their plan to build the finest ground in the country.

XYZ Rovers press on with their plan to build the finest team in the country.

Marshmallow Wanderers press on regardless, having had no practicable proposals submitted in response to their requests, except for one which they do not care to mention.

The Monopolies Commission issues an interim report on the complaint, first lodged in 1956, that two League teams were playing respectively a robot centre forward and a robot goalkeeper, both made by the same electronics firm. The problem, the Commission states, is now complicated by a further complaint about a non-League team which is alleged to consist entirely of eleven brothers. This, it points out, if true, is an even more blatant example of manufacturing monopoly.

The crystal glows green, which may mean that Spring is on the way, or may mean that envy and uncharitableness are splitting the ranks of footballers as the season grows older.

Ground conditions certainly improve. As grounds become better, more players are ordered off them. A famous referee says: 'It's not that players are any dirtier — it's just that they've no longer got the excuse that they couldn't stop in time.'

Spring is in the air. Those who do not spring in the air smartly enough when facing the stalwart defenders of Cumberthwaite Cloggers FC are good-humouredly kicked in t'air.

'The Sickness of British Football' says a newspaper headline. 'High Pay — Low Standards — Corruption — Incompetent Administration.' Blissfully unaware of all this, hundreds of thousands of innocent young men continue to play the game week by week, apparently for the odd reason that they enjoy it.

A national newspaper selects its ideal England team. This brings the total of different players nominated by the Press for the England team during the season to 250. Mr Alf Ramsey publicly thanks the Press for its interest, but points out that international rules stipulate that only eleven men can represent a country on the field at any one time.

Before the transfer deadline ends in March, four First Division clubs pay out over £80,000 each for star forwards.

A Second Division club pays out £70,000 for a star defender.

Marshmallow Wanderers, after a whip-round among the Committee, pay out 1/3d. for a tin of dubbin.

On 1 April Cumberthwaite Cloggers announce the transfer of a star from Real Madrid. Twice the normal crowd turns up to see this deadline-beating attraction. All fifty of them meet him personally, as he turns out to be Real's star peanut-vendor.

An inexperienced sports writer is reprimanded by his editor for writing a straightforward account of a football match, with no reference to what the players said to the referee, or what the managers said to the players at half-time, or why the visiting centre-forward's fiancée spent the afternoon eating meat pies at Wigan airport. He is transferred to a spell of political reporting to improve his imagination.

The 630th Football League club manager to do so since the war parts with his club. After treatment with a truth drug he says: 'I was sacked.' If all the football managers to lose their jobs since the war were laid end to end on green benches they would closely resemble the members of the House of Commons.

The American State Department releases the news that three cosmonauts from Cape Kennedy have been seconded to fill current managerial vacancies with English football clubs. It is understood that this constitutes part of their training for going into orbit.

Sensational news. As the season draws to its close, it is announced that a well-known organization specialising in opinion polls has programmed its electronic computer to come up with the result of the FA Cup Final before the game is played. This is intended as a dummy run in preparation for the forecasting of the next General Election result.

The Monopolies Commission issues an interim addendum to its interim report. The problem, it seems is even more complicated than it appeared to be, because the eleven brothers about whom complaint was made turn out to be the football team representing a famous monastery …

Mr Alf Ramsey, contemplating the large number of people who, during the season, have voluntarily done his job as England team manager for him, generously decides to share out his salary equally among them. Unfortunately the gesture is made meaningless by the fact that the farthing is no longer legal tender.

The crystal, glowing red from overwork, has one more revelation to reveal. After many days of anxious nationwide speculation, the electronic computer delivers, twenty-four hours before the match, the result of the English FA Cup Final at Wembley. It is:

Kilmarnock 1, Labour Party 378.

Shamrock Rovers demand a recount.

After this the cracker slips give out, the crystal gives up, and so do I.

A thrashing for West Ham at Bramall Lane. Sheffield United centre-forward, Mick Jones, heads in his team's fifth goal.

Their Story: Tranmere Rovers

Despite their modest performances in League and Cup the name of Tranmere Rovers appears in all the record books.

On Boxing Day, 1935 they rattled up thirteen goals against Oldham Athletic. Oldham replied with four. No other League match before or after has produced an aggregate of seventeen goals. And only one other club has scored as many as thirteen — Stockport County, who beat Halifax Town 13–0 in 1934.

The Tranmere club was started by some young Birkenhead cricketers in 1883, and became founder members of the Liverpool and District League. Later they joined the Lancashire Combination, and won the Championship in 1908. Four years later they moved to the present ground in Prenton Park. After playing for a couple of seasons in the Central League, they became one of the original members of the Third Division (North) when it began in 1921.

They improved gradually from a modest start, and headed the table for a time in the 1923–4 season. There was some reason for this, as they had in their side a youngster of sixteen who was destined to become one of the greatest centre forwards of all time.

His name was 'Dixie' Dean.

Unfortunately for the Cheshire club they could not afford to keep him for long despite gates of ten thousand and more. The following year he moved to Everton, and Tranmere sank to last but one in the League.

Soon they found another great leader — Tommy ('Pongo') Waring, who later moved to Aston Villa and became an England inter-national. If they could not do much else, Tranmere could certainly discover centre forwards in those days.

In 1935 things at last began to stir at Prenton Park. Again a star centre forward helped Tranmere to success — Bunny Bell. He scored nine of those thirteen goals against Oldham, an individual goal-scoring record for the League until it was beaten by Joe Payne of Luton, who scored ten against Bristol Rovers later in the same season.

Bell scored 35 goals for Tranmere in 1933–4 and 33 in 1935–6. Like Dean, he later moved to Everton, but was never capped for his country.

Tranmere finished third in the League in 1935–6, and they also made one of their infrequent appearances in the Fourth Round of the FA Cup. In the Third Round they had beaten Notts County 4–3 after a replay, and more than 22,000 fans crowded into Prenton Park to see the game against Barnsley.

They were disappointed. Tranmere lost 4–2.

But they did not have to wait much longer for Tranmere's outstanding season. In 1937–8 the club did not concede more than two goals in any match. They had a formidable defence with goalkeeper Jack Curnow and centre half Archie Clarke outstanding. They finished top of the League, and up they went.

After such a long wait for success everyone on Merseyside hoped their stay in the Second Division would be a long one. It couldn't have been shorter. They had a disastrous time, winning only six games and finishing with 17 points — 14 fewer than the club just above them. Back they went to the Third Division.

After the War they never threatened to return; in fact, they were often struggling to avoid having to apply for re-election. In spite of this they had some fine players, among whom was Harold Bell. Between 1946 and 1955 he played in every League match, making 401 consecutive appearances.

In 1953 the great Spurs team came to Birkenhead in the Third Round of the FA Cup, and were held to a draw. Tranmere were actually leading at half time, but could not hold out. In the replay they were beaten 9–1.

Although Tranmere did not have to play in the Fourth Division when it was formed in 1958, they dropped down to it three seasons later. In 1963 they hit the headlines by holding Chelsea to a draw at home in the Fourth Round of the FA Cup, only to lose in London 3–1.

Last season they made a determined effort to get promotion. They had an experienced winger in Alan A'Court, a former England international, and goalscoring Barry Dyson and John Manning in the forward line. They strengthened the team by buying players with First Division experience like Bruce Crawford from Blackpool, but after a thrilling tussle with Torquay, Darlington, Doncaster and Colchester they just failed to get back to Division Three.

In the pre-season game at Prenton Park, Ralph Brand, recently transferred to Manchester City from Glasgow Rangers, turns the ball just the wrong side of the post when challenged by King, the Tranmere half-back.

STARS OF SCOTLAND

Left: Jim Baxter of Sunderland *(on extreme right)* tries to evade the Nottingham Forest 'keeper, Peter Grummitt.

Bottom left: Denis Law, skipper of Manchester United, leads out his team.

Bottom right: Pat Crerand, his club colleague, in determined mood.

Modern Tactics

Brian Marshall

Revolutionary coaching and training methods are changing the whole concept of patterns of play in soccer. At both international and club level a high degree of planning is apparent in all the top sides.

The most common playing style to flourish in recent seasons has been the 4–2–4 system. This formation has proved ideal for teams who, perhaps lacking great individual skill, have been able to win honours by the clever use of available talent. The success of West Ham United and Liverpool comes to mind.

Both clubs possess astute managers. Ron Greenwood at Upton Park, formerly Arsenal's chief coach, and Bill Shankly at Anfield are acknowledged to be two of the most dedicated managers in soccer today, and they devote a great deal of thought to the technical side of the game.

They only sign players whom they are sure will fit into their team policy. This was demonstrated at Liverpool with the signing of Geoff Strong. Although Strong played at inside right for most of his stay at Highbury, Shankly had no hesitation in switching him to wing half when England half-back Gordon Milne suffered the first of his series of injuries.

Both clubs have achieved success in European soccer by keeping up with the times. Messrs Greenwood and Shankly have done some hard thinking. And they favour the 4–2–4 system, or some variation of it.

In this formation there are four strong-tackling back men (two looking after the middle), two creative link men operating in mid-field to fetch and carry, and four front players all capable of scoring goals.

4–2–4, which encourages the retreating defence, first appeared in Spain. It was originally devised to cut out the danger created by fast, swooping wingers like Gento. No doubt Helenio Herrera, who transformed Barcelona into an outstanding team, played a leading part in its introduction.

Under the old W formation, with deep-lying inside forwards, a most profitable move was the long cross-field pass by the inside forward to his opposite winger. To prevent this form of attack culminating in a goal, the defenders had to follow a set pattern.

If the outside left gained possession the right back would be drawn to the wing. The centre half would be pulled out of position to fill the gap created by the full back's move. This often resulted in the centre forward being unmarked, as the left back would be unable to provide adequate cover.

But the 4–2–4 defensive line-up, with its two centre backs, gives an additional safeguard against such a move.

This plan to combat fast wingers has now been further developed to such a degree that its highly successful formation is used by almost every League club in the country.

Yet it is still a relative innovation in England.

Brazil, one of the main exponents of the method, won the World Cup in Sweden in 1958 after adopting it. England's former team manager, Walter Winterbottom, an outstanding tactician, was unable to experiment with the system until two years later.

He took the plunge in an international match against Spain, after he had seen Ron Flowers successfully combat the tactics of two Yugoslav attacking forwards in the previous game. The move did not prove a success on this particular occasion, mainly because the task of keeping a player like di Stefano quiet was a mammoth one in itself.

But the important thing was that England were at last developing a modern style of play. Defenders were learning not to stake everything on desperate tackles. They discovered that to outwit an opponent by retreating was an advantageous move. The only time to tackle was when they thought they had more than an even chance of emerging with the ball.

By this policy of defending in numbers (the 'blanket' defence), they built up a strong barrier that opposing teams found difficult to penetrate.

It is, however, at club level that the success of this ultra-defensive policy has paid rich dividends. A case in point is the winning of the European Cup-Winners' Cup by West Ham in 1965, when they defeated Munich at Wembley by two Alan Sealey goals in two minutes.

The London club play the 4–2–4 plan regardless of the opposition. At full strength they are an effective side with specialist players carrying out their allotted roles with effortless ease. Against Munich they showed what a high standard of performance can be achieved with this method.

With skipper Bobby Moore making vital sorties upfield to relieve the monotony, West Ham held the initiative throughout. Their defensive play early in the second half paved the way for victory, and it was during this period that 4–2–4 was seen in its best light.

When Munich did occasionally break clear they found goalkeeper Jim Standen in fine form. He would advance confidently to cut off the through pass after the West Ham defenders had methodically retreated to plan.

Another game in which this formation was used to full advantage was one between Moscow Dynamo and Walsall at Fellows Park. The Russian team took a second-minute lead through their link man Maslov, who was wearing the number five shirt, incidentally.

After gaining this quick advantage Dynamo slowly slipped back on the defensive, using 4–2–4. Although Walsall quickly recovered from their setback they could make no headway; they were given plenty of room to work the ball in midfield, but ran into a solid wall of resistance on the edge of the penalty area.

After the interval Dynamo broke through with a series of snap breakaways. Walsall, who were playing the conventional 2–3–5 line-up were caught sadly out of position, and in the final quarter of an hour the Russians scored four times through Schivtsev (2) and Gusarov (2).

On every occasion it was the quick break that gave Dynamo a goal. Only two Russian players were usually involved in Walsall's half of the field, supporting the view that over eighty-five per cent of goals scored in competitive matches come from moves of three passes or fewer.

The controversial 4–3–3 line-up (really a variation of 4–2–4) is a formation that can only be operated successfully by teams made up of individualists working together to form an effective combination.

The additional player in mid-field instead of in the front line means that there are no wingers in the conventional sense. The three front players must operate over the full width of the field.

Once again Brazil have perfected the method. Of course with Pele in their side they have an unique player. He is one of the few footballers in the world capable of beating a string of opponents over a distance of fifty yards, and then finishing off the movement himself with a spectacular shot at goal.

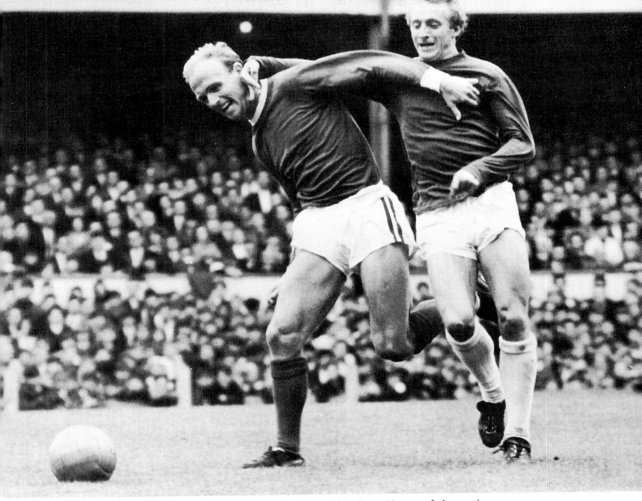

Denis Law *(right)* — striker and schemer — in a tussle with Don Howe of Arsenal.

In Britain perhaps the best 4–3–3 club example is Manchester United, where the trio of David Herd, Bobby Charlton and Denis Law make up a fine attacking combination.

Law is both striker and schemer, and his versatile skill has made United one of the most attractive teams in the country.

England's present team manager, Alf Ramsey, experimented with 4–3–3 in the international match against Spain in Madrid last season. His surprise selection was the inclusion of Alan Ball, Blackpool's inside forward, on the right wing. Ball did not play a winger's role; instead he was given a roving commission in midfield, and did much to inspire a fine tactical victory for England.

In this formation full backs George Cohen and Ray Wilson had to share in attacks. Wilson, in fact, provided the pass from which England scored their first goal.

He picked up a pass following a George Eastham free kick, and raced down the left flank before putting across a short centre from which Joe Baker scored.

England's success in this game proved that the 4–3–3 plan does not require standard wingers — ironically, the very players that the 4–2–4 system was devised to eliminate as an attacking force.

In contrast 4–3–3 can be operated to exploit a strong defence. It calls for fluidity by all members of the side to take an attacking role if and when required.

Joe Shaw, long-serving Sheffield United defender, and the ideal 'sweeper.'

This is why terms like full back, wing half and forwards are beginning to be old fashioned. Now we hear of strikers, link men — and the sweeper. The latter is a new term to describe the function of one player in defence.

He operates behind the normal defence division, and if any opponents do penetrate the defensive line it is his job to provide a second challenge as quickly as possible. He must also take up the position of any of the four men in front of him when they move up into the attack.

Joe Shaw of Sheffield United is an ideal sweeper, and it is not without significance that with the inclusion of Shaw the Yorkshire club have had one of the best defensive records in the last few years. The sweeper can be employed in both 4–2–4 and 4–3–3 systems. Many clubs vary their formation from one to the other of these methods according to the state of the game and the strength and weaknesses of the opposition.

Provided they have the players who thoroughly understand their roles in each, of course.

Managers who encourage these modern tactics must acquire players who are ready and willing to learn; there is far more specialisation in football today than ever before.

It is, however, the fresh thinking of soccer coaches that has changed the whole concept of the game. When these coaches assume the responsibilities of managers then they can really put their ideas into practice.

And this, in turn, has forced the players themselves to think more deeply about the game both on and off the field.

The only section of the football world who appears to be lagging behind are the spectators.

They have yet to be convinced that success in modern football has to be built on a strong defence, and that 4–2–4 and 4–3–3 represent the best methods yet devised of achieving it.

Substitutes — So Far, So Good

Perhaps the most surprising thing about it was that the Football League tackled the difficult question of substitutes at all.

The second most influential body in soccer in this country is not renowned for progressive thinking. In the early years of the European Cup competition they actually ordered the League Champions, Manchester United, not to take part.

The Football League decided that in the 1965–6 season if a player was injured in a League match he could be replaced by a substitute named before the kick-off. Only one such substitution was allowed; if another player of the same side subsequently went off injured the team would have to carry on with ten men.

Ruling bodies in some sports, although no doubt acting in what they think are their game's best interests, are sometimes too prone to meddle with the Laws. An obvious example is the MCC, who, in an endeavour to keep the balance between bat and ball in cricket, are always passing experimental Laws about bowlers' front feet, preparing pitches, polishing balls and all the rest of it. These changes have often done no more than confuse cricketers and spectators alike.

They have not, however changed the Law concerning substitutes, who can field but cannot bat or bowl.

It has taken a long time for the burning question of substitutes in competitive soccer matches to be tackled.

The majority of the Cup-finals between 1952 and 1960 were ruined by injuries to players. No substitutes were allowed, and of the eight teams that had a player injured at some stage in those Finals, six of them lost. Yet substitutes are still not permitted in FA Cup matches.

Ten men gallantly struggling against the

At first there was confusion. John Holsgrove of Wolves does not know whether to come on or not when colleague David Wagstaffe is injured. Referee Hamer tries to help.

odds may be a stirring sight, but there is no doubt that those ten men are under a severe handicap. If they have to play against eleven for long they are bound to tire first, and will need a lot of luck to avoid defeat.

Some people say that substitutes take the chance element out of soccer, but spectators pay their entrance money to see a contest fought out by eleven men on each side for the full ninety minutes. Chance comes into soccer all the time; a slip, a lucky bounce of the ball, the angle at which it hits the woodwork. It does not have to include a player being injured and carried off, leaving his side a man short.

The named substitute is usually a utility player — one who can play anywhere. Except in goal. When a goalkeeper is injured he has to be replaced by a non-specialist in that position, so his team is still handicapped in spite of having eleven players.

Apart from this the new rule has done a lot to redress the balance.

Has it been abused?

Well, in the intense struggle for League points it is obvious that there will have been instances when a tired, off-form or only slightly-injured player has been told that 'his strained muscle is not standing up to match-play' and quietly led off the field, limping badly, to be replaced by a fresh man.

This is the sort of thing that legislators are afraid of.

There is no doubt that sorely-pressed managers might be tempted to take advantage of an opportunity to substitute one player for another. Yet a manager chooses what he thinks is the best team for the particular match; his substitute may be a useful man, but he has not been the first choice for any position that day.

Will managers often indulge in malpractices like replacing fit players? After all the word will soon get round — the player himself knows perfectly well if he is fit to continue or not, and if he is told to leave the field when he is all right he won't like it.

Players can't be treated today as they were twenty years ago; anyone who gets that sort of order from the manager will soon be asking for a transfer.

League soccer is a spectator sport. The crowds must somehow be tempted back into the soccer grounds on Saturday afternoons instead of cluttering up the shopping centres with their cars or gazing at the telly.

Our climate does not help; the facilities provided on many grounds are woeful. The game itself must be the attraction.

Standing in the rain on open terraces or sitting on a hard seat in an unheated stand, spectators must be kept so enthralled by what is going on in the middle that they forget their miserable watching conditions.

One team battling hopelessly with ten men is not likely to encourage them to continue to come, or attract others.

The Football League have certainly shown unaccustomed boldness in trying to tackle the difficult problem of substitutes. The one-substitute rule is better than the no-substitute rule. Have they gone far enough?

Well, nobody wants to see a new forward line coming out every few minutes as in ice hockey, but the League's compromise plan does not completely solve the problem.

The rule must be extended to allow a second goalkeeper to be named in case of injury to the original one.

And perhaps the number of permitted substitutes could be increased, provided some laid-down period of time elapses between an injured player leaving the field and his replacement coming on.

This would mean that a player would not go off unless he was genuinely injured because his team would be a man short for that period.

Ingenious people are always devising ways of getting round Laws, but it would seem that few managers would be likely to risk playing a man short deliberately in order to replace a player who was not quite up to form.

48

Picture Quiz—1

Who are these players?

Left: The former Charlton captain and right half, who was transferred to Wolves last year for a fee of £40,000.

Bottom left: Preston's strong-shooting centre forward, who has played for Preston and Manchester United in FA Cup-finals.

Bottom right: Sunderland and Eire centre half, and one of the best defenders in League soccer.

Don't look up the answers yet. There is another Picture Quiz on page 89.

Star of the future. Peter Osgood (*right*) tackled by John Sjoberg of Leicester City.

Just as many Goals

Dennis Smith

'Newcastle United 0, Liverpool 0; Notting-ham Forest 0, Sunderland 0; Sheffield Wednesday 0, West Ham United 0; West Bromwich Albion 0, . . .'

My father tossed his newspaper away in disgust.

'I don't know what they bother to play for,' he grumbled. 'I thought they were supposed to score goals in soccer. No wonder the attendances keep going down.'

'Didn't you get those draws on your coupon?' I asked innocently.

He ignored that. Obviously he hadn't.

'Of the fourteen teams playing in the First Division yesterday nine of them failed to score a single goal.'

'One match was abandoned just after half-time.'

My father snorted. 'They probably wouldn't have scored if they'd still been playing.'

'Lots of mud,' I suggested.

'What's that got to do with it? When I used to watch a game of football we saw some action — some goals. We wouldn't have been content to put up with those nine-men-in-defence tactics that all the teams seem to rely on these days. In my day a forward stayed up the field, not in his own penalty area . . .'

I sighed. We'd had all this before.

I thought that he was going to say that in those days the weather was so good that the grounds never got muddy, but perhaps that was in the cricket season. Well, I'd have to tell him.

'I'm afraid you're wrong there, Dad,' I began. 'There are just as many goals scored

in First Division soccer today as there were when you watched it thirty years ago.'

'That's nonsense!' he said. 'When was the club goal-scoring record set up? Aston Villa did it in 1930–1, didn't they? 128 goals. And Arsenal, the Champions, got one fewer.'

'That's quite true,' I replied, 'but that was an exceptional season. Over 1800 goals were scored in the First Division that year. It hadn't been done before, and hasn't been done since.'

'Arsenal got 118 when they won the Championship for the third time in succession two years later,' went on my father. 'What a forward line they had — Joe Hulme, David Jack, Jack Lambert, Alex James and Cliff Bastin.'

The old chap had a nostalgic look on his face. He'd always been an Arsenal supporter. But I'd have to bring him down to earth.

I'm rather keen on soccer statistics, and I'd mugged this lot up only the other day so I was well briefed.

'As a matter of fact,' I told him, 'more goals were scored in the First Division in 1960–1 than in the year you're talking about. 1724 compared with 1645 in the same number of matches.'

My father looked surprised.

'There's no statistical evidence whatsoever to prove that League soccer is becoming more defensive. The average number of goals per match is very nearly the same now as it was after the offside rule was altered in 1925. Before that, of course, there were many fewer — that's why they changed the Law.'

'I would have thought that might be the case in the lower Divisions, but not in Division One.'

'Wrong again, Dad,' I laughed. 'The average of goals per match is actually higher in top-class football. The goal-scoring ability of players like Denis Law, Jimmy Greaves and others is reflected in these figures. Division One defenders are better footballers than those in Division Four, but they're not able to prevent goals with the same ease because their opponents are more skilful.'

'The inference is, then, that if 4–2–4, the blanket defence and all the rest hadn't been invented we'd have had a feast of goals?'

'Yes, we probably would. Then they would probably have had to change the game by legislation again. Of course, the Italians are the masters of defensive soccer. Compared with their matches, most of ours produce a glut of goals.'

'No wonder the spectators there throw things.'

I was beginning to warm up.

'On one Saturday in October last season the eleven First Division games produced an aggregate of 48 goals. That's not bad — let's see, 4·36 per match, isn't it?'

I could see my father was beginning to tire.

'That's well above the average. Over the whole season it will probably be about 3·5 or 3·6.'

He'd picked up the newspaper again.

'Dundee United 0, Kilmarnock 0' he said. 'I got that one down for a draw.'

There's no stopping this one! Pat Liney, St. Mirren goalie, does his best but he has no chance with this fine shot from the boot of Glasgow Rangers' centre forward, Jim Forrest.

Honours Board

This order of merit is based on the principal honours gained by clubs that are at present members of the Football League. Points are halved for honours shared.

	Football League				FA Cup		Losing Semi-Finalists	FA Charity Shield	Total
	Division 1		Division 2		Finalists				
	1st	2nd	1st	2nd	Winners	Losers			
Points awarded	4	3	2	1	4	2	1	1	18
Aston Villa	24	24	4	—	28	4	8	—	92
Manchester United	24	18	2	4	12	4	6	4½	74½
Everton	24	18	2	1	12	6	7	3	73
Arsenal	28	6	—	1	12	6	3	7	63
Wolverhampton Wanderers	12	15	2	—	16	8	2	2½	57½
Liverpool	28	6	8	—	4	4	5	1	56
Preston North End	8	18	6	2	8	10	3	—	55
Newcastle United	16	—	2	2	24	8	2	1	55
Sheffield Wednesday	16	3	10	1	12	4	8	1	55
Sunderland	24	15	—	1	4	2	7	1	54
Tottenham Hotspur	8	12	4	2	16	—	4	4	50
West Bromwich Albion	4	6	4	2	16	10	6	1½	49½
Blackburn Rovers	8	—	2	1	24	4	8	1	48
Manchester City	4	6	12	2	12	6	2	1	45
Sheffield United	4	6	2	3	16	4	4	—	39
Huddersfield Town	12	9	—	2	4	8	2	1	38
Bolton Wanderers	—	—	2	4	16	6	5	—	33
Derby County	—	9	4	1	4	6	8	—	32
Burnley	8	6	2	2	4	4	4	½	30½
Nottingham Forest	—	—	4	1	8	—	7	—	20
Leicester City	—	3	8	1	—	6	1	—	19
Portsmouth	8	—	—	1	4	4	1	½	18½
Birmingham City	—	—	8	2	—	4	4	—	18
Chelsea	4	—	—	4	—	2	7	1	18
Leeds United	—	6	4	3	—	2	—	—	15
Blackpool	—	3	2	1	4	4	—	—	14
Cardiff City	—	3	—	3	4	2	1	1	14
Notts County	—	—	4	1	4	2	2	—	13
Bury	—	—	2	1	8	—	—	—	11
West Ham United	—	—	2	1	4	2	1	½	10½
Charlton Athletic	—	3	—	1	4	2	—	—	10
Southampton	—	—	—	1	—	4	5	—	10
Bristol City	—	3	2	—	—	2	1	—	8
Fulham	—	—	2	1	—	—	4	—	7
Grimsby Town	—	—	4	1	—	—	2	—	7
Barnsley	—	—	—	—	4	2	—	—	6
Bradford City	—	—	2	—	4	—	—	—	6
Ipswich Town	4	—	2	—	—	—	—	—	6
Stoke City	—	—	4	1	—	—	1	—	5
Middlesbrough	—	—	4	1	—	—	—	—	5
Oldham Athletic	—	3	—	1	—	—	1	—	5
Luton Town	—	—	—	1	—	2	—	—	3
Millwall	—	—	—	—	—	—	3	—	3
Brentford	—	—	2	—	—	—	—	—	2
Swindon Town	—	—	—	—	—	—	2	—	2
Swansea Town	—	—	—	—	—	—	2	—	2
Bradford	—	—	—	1	—	—	—	—	1
Crewe Alexandra	—	—	—	—	—	—	1	—	1
Hull City	—	—	—	—	—	—	1	—	1
Norwich City	—	—	—	—	—	—	1	—	1
Port Vale	—	—	—	—	—	—	1	—	1
Reading	—	—	—	—	—	—	1	—	1
York City	—	—	—	—	—	—	1	—	1
Leyton Orient	—	—	—	1	—	—	—	—	1
Northampton Town	—	—	—	1	—	—	—	—	1

Moving Around

Derek Dougan

Some of my footballing friends have stayed with one League club throughout their playing careers. Johnny Haynes of Fulham, for example, and Bryan Douglas of Blackburn Rovers. Well, good luck to them — they've obviously been happy, so why make a change?

Perhaps I've got a restless nature. I don't think I could have stayed put anywhere for twenty years however pleasant the surroundings were.

Playing in the south, north and midlands of England, as well as in Northern Ireland as a home-team player has given me a wealth of experience. I'd never have got it by appearing a few times a year in those regions as a member of a visiting side.

You don't get the feel of a place in a few hours — or a few weeks. You have to live there, and get to know the people.

I suppose I owe my start in soccer to Mr. Mawhinney, the sportsmaster in my Belfast school. I don't know why he picked on me to play football except that I could run pretty fast. But I took to the game at once, practised hard, and played whenever I could in any position that came my way.

When I left school I joined the Irish League club, Distillery, and from there I came to Portsmouth in 1957. While I was with Pompey I had the honour of being chosen to go to Sweden for the 1958 World Cup-finals with the Northern Ireland party.

I did not think I would get the chance of playing, but I was picked as centre forward for the first game against Czechoslovakia. Earlier in the season I had played for Northern Ireland's B side against Rumania, and had scored three of our six goals.

I think I was the youngest player in the competition that year with the exception of that soccer genius from Brazil, Pelé. And I was probably the most nervous, too.

We beat the Czechs 1–0, with a goal by Willie Cush, and went on to reach the Quarter-finals before being beaten 4–0 by France.

My next move took me to Lancashire. In 1959 I joined Blackburn Rovers, and the following year paid my first visit to Wembley Stadium. We reached the final of the FA Cup, and met Wolverhampton Wanderers.

Seven of the previous eight Cup-finals at Wembley had been marred by injuries to players. We could not help thinking that one of us might be carried off this time.

Our fears were realised only too well. Dave Whelan, our left back, broke his leg a minute before half-time.

No substitute was allowed, and we soon found the odds too great.

Substitutes are now allowed in League games, but not in the FA Cup. The biggest match of the season, with a hundred thousand people in the ground and millions watching on television, can still be ruined as a spectacle by an unlucky accident to a player.

We lost 3–0, as we were almost bound to do with a handicap like that.

My next move was to Aston Villa, where I stayed for two seasons. Then I had a new experience — a spell of Third Division football with Peterborough United, who had only

Leicester City *versus* Leeds United. Derek watches Billy Bremner and Gary Sprake clear his header following a corner kick.

been elected to the League in 1960, and had won promotion at their first attempt.

Here I found there was not so much emphasis on pure football. Skill there was, but physical strength played a bigger part in success than it did in the top class.

I thoroughly enjoyed my stay with Peterborough, especially during our great FA Cup run in 1964–5. As a non-League club Peterborough had often performed giant-killing feats, and were no strangers to the Fourth Round after playing through the Preliminary Competition.

But when we drew Arsenal at home there was terrific excitement in the town.

I'll never forget that game.

Arsenal were winning 1–0, when I picked up a pass from Ronnie Barnes, feinted to go one way and went the other, completely surprising Ian Ure, the Arsenal centre-half. I shot hard, and I don't think I've ever felt better in my life than when I saw that ball go into the net.

We played above ourselves, and later on Peter McNamee scored a second goal for us. The crowd went wild with delight. Moments like this stay in your memory for ever.

Like Walsall before us, we had toppled mighty Arsenal.

In the Fifth Round for the first time in the club's history we beat Swansea Town 2–0 after the first match had ended in a goalless draw. We had Wembley in our sights, but in the last Round in which we could be asked to play on our opponents' ground our luck ran out.

We had to come to Stamford Bridge, where Chelsea easily beat us 5—1.

In the summer of 1965 I came back to the First Division with a new club — Leicester City. To be honest I was glad to be playing top-class soccer again. For one thing I could try and win back my place in the Northern Ireland side — the hurly-burly of Third Division football is not really the place to be if you want to be considered for international matches.

I was lucky to get an early opportunity to show what I could do.

It is always a great feeling for an Irishman to run on to the field at Windsor Park, Belfast wearing the green jersey of his country.

Derek scores Leicester's second goal against Chelsea at Stamford Bridge. Terry Venables holds his face in despair as Derek is congratulated by his happy colleagues. Leicester won 2—0.

National pride helps to spur on every player in the side to superhuman effort.

That's why results often do not run to form, and many highly-praised teams from abroad have been forced to admit defeat.

My come-back was in last season's game against Scotland played there. I was playing at inside left in the role of striker, with Burnley's Willie Irvine in the middle.

We were soon one down — Alan Gilzean heading in from Willie Henderson's centre — but in no way disheartened by that. Plenty of chances come along in ninety minutes' football.

Just before half-time George Best appeared to be fouled in the area by a Scottish defender, and I half stopped, expecting the whistle to be blown for a penalty.

Nothing happened. But the ball ran loose to me about eighteen yards out.

I thumped it as hard as I could, and saw it crash against the underside of the bar and enter the net. What a moment!

Soon after the interval Johnny Crossan gave us the lead, only for Gilzean to level the scores eight minutes from the finish.

A desperate struggle ensued for the winner. Then came a great moment for the Irish.

Jimmy McIlroy took a free kick way out on the right wing, and floated the ball towards the near post where I was waiting for it. I headed it back on to the six-yard line, and Irvine, falling backwards, hooked in an overhead shot that completely beat the Scottish 'keeper.

It was a happy return to international football for me. A few weeks later we met England, and lost a rather drab match 2—1. Wembley doesn't seem to be a very lucky ground for me; both my appearances there have ended in disappointment.

That's soccer all over. Experience has taught me that you must never get bigheaded when things are going your way nor become unduly depressed when they aren't. Things like that are all in the game.

A move to another club often helps when the ball just doesn't run for you. Then you get a new zest for the game, make new friends, see different places, and most probably regain your touch.

Willie Irvine's overhead shot that won the match for Ireland.

Puzzle Page (Answers on Page 128.)

1 Odd Team Out
In each of the following groups one of the clubs is in some way different from the others.

Can you spot who they are, and say why they are different?

(1) Burnley, Everton, Sheffield Wednesday, Stoke City.

(2) Fulham, Luton Town, Derby County, Norwich City.

(3) Bradford City, Nottingham Forest, Middlesbrough, Portsmouth.

(4) Brentford, Grimsby Town, Coventry City, Wolverhampton Wanderers.

2 Splitting the Names
A well-known soccer player is hidden in each of the sentences below. All you have to do is to put together two of the words in each sentence to make the name of the player.

(1) 'That fellow is a jolly good player.'

(2) The new coal bin will hold an extra ton.

(3) The man chose a pen with a fine nib.

(4) There was a nasty burn on the right side of his face.

(5) The tulip field was simply a mass of bloom.

(6) 'Please send the car into town today for the luggage.'

3 Who Scored?
'Who scored the winning goal today?' asked Bill.

'The centre-forward,' said Joe.

'No, it was the outside right,' said Harry.

'One of the half-backs,' contradicted Bert.

'Yes, that's correct,' said Don. 'The right-half.'

'You mean the left half,' said Mike.

'It was definitely one of the forwards,' said Dave.

'Yes, the inside left,' said Tony.

'The inside-right,' put in Arthur.

'I'm sure it was the outside left,' said John.

In fact only *one* of these remarks was correct. Can you discover who made it, and then help Bill to find out who did score the winning goal that day?

4 Noughts and Crosses
Replace the noughts and crosses below to make six-letter words which fit the clues. If you do this correctly you will find that the diagonal line of noughts is replaced by the name of a Scottish League club.

o x x x x x Leeds United and England wing half.

x o x x x x An accurate one may lead to a goal.

x x o x x x Chelsea inside forward.

x x x o x x Fourth Division side.

x x x x o x Their job is to find good players.

x x x x x o Queen's Park Rangers play in this road.

5 Players and Clubs
There are five players named Brown, Hart, Lewis, Milton and Williams. Their clubs are Burnley, Huddersfield Town, Liverpool, Manchester United and West Ham United.

None of these players plays for a club whose name begins with the same letter as his own name.

Lewis's club won the FA Cup in 1963, Milton's the following year and Hart's the year after that.

For whom does Williams play?

6 Goal Average
Railton City had a good season. Out of the twelve matches played they won four 3–1, three 2–0 and two 2–1.

Two others ended in one-all draws, and they were beaten 1–0 in their final game.

What was their goal average at the end of the season?

A desperate struggle for possession between George Armstrong of Arsenal (No. 7) and Fulham's Rodney Marsh

Spotlight on Cliff Jones

If anyone can be said to have soccer in the blood it's Cliff Jones.

His father, Ivor, played for Swansea, West Bromwich Albion and Aldershot; his uncle, Bryn, for Wolves, Arsenal and Norwich City. Both were Welsh internationals. Right from the start young Cliff was brought up to believe that he would be a footballer, too, and as soon as he was old enough he joined Swansea Town.

He played for the League side when he was seventeen, displacing his brother Bryn at inside right. Later he moved to outside left, and had Ivor Allchurch as his partner. When he returned from his Army service he felt that he had got as far as he could at Vetch Field, and asked for a transfer.

There were plenty of clubs anxious to sign this versatile player, and in February 1958 he joined Spurs. The fee was £35,000 — a record at that time. Before the next season began he broke a leg in practice, and was out of the game for several months.

Cliff Jones played a vital part in all the great Spurs' triumphs — the Cup and League double in 1961, the Cup again the following year and the European Cup-winners' Cup in 1963.

Many players can run fast; many can control the ball well. But not all that many can do both together. Cliff can control the ball while moving at great speed, thrilling the crowd with his swerving gallops. When he sets off on one of these inspired runs from mid-field nobody knows which way he is going — least of all his opponents — and when his effort seems to have spent itself and he is surrounded by three or four defenders, he'll dodge and feint and be off again at top speed towards goal.

But he's not just a runner and a dribbler. He can centre the ball accurately, put in a snap shot from a moving ball and is expert in seizing a half-chance. And he is equally at home on the right or left wing.

Cliff Jones first played for Wales in 1954 against Austria, and was an automatic choice for his country for the next decade. In the following year Wales beat England 2–1 — and young Cliff got the winning goal. It was Wales's first victory over England since 1938, when Bryn Jones scored one of their four goals.

In the matter of injuries Jones has not been the luckiest of players; his style of play has made him the recipient of some heavy tackles.

Before last season began he injured a hamstring muscle while playing in Spain, and then broke down again in a friendly match in September.

It was more than three months before he played his first League game — against Burnley at Turf Moor — and a week later the cries of 'There goes Cliff!' rang out again at White Hart Lane as he set off on yet another of his dazzling runs. Cliff Jones responded with two well-taken goals, and helped Spurs to a 4–2 win over Chelsea.

Later in the season he was injured again, and there is no doubt that the moderate performance of Tottenham Hotspur in the League last year was in no small measure due to the absence of their talented and experienced Welsh international winger.

Cliff Jones in action. *Above:* Being congratulated after scoring his second goal against Chelsea. *Below:* A spectacular scissors kick in the match against Everton. It went just wide, and the game ended in a 2—2 draw.

Their Story: Notts County

Notts County is the oldest League club. It was founded more than a hundred years ago – in 1862, the year before the Football Association was founded and soccer officially born.

The club was formed by a famous cricketer, Richard Daft, and a number of other 'fellows of the better class socially' as they were described at the time, and they played their matches on the county cricket ground at Trent Bridge.

One of their players, Greenhalgh, was picked for England in the very first international match against Scotland in 1872 'for the very important position of three-quarter back' according to a writer of the time, who went on to explain that he was 'the man whose special duty it is to give the goalkeeper assistance.' He must have performed well because the game ended in a goalless draw.

Notts County were among the twelve clubs that founded the Football League in 1888, and they remained in the top Division for five years. Then they had a spell of four seasons in Division Two, during which time they became the first Second Division club to win the FA Cup.

Logan's match, they called it. He scored three goals in the County's 4–1 win over Bolton Wanderers, and would have got many more if it had not been for the brilliant goalkeeping of John Sutcliffe, Bolton's international goalkeeper.

Apart from Logan, County's many fine players of the time included skipper David Calderhead, a hard-tackling centre half, and their amateur outside left H. B. Daft, who helped the Corinthians to many of their great victories over the professional clubs.

This was Notts County's one and only FA Cup triumph. Since then they have never got further than the Semi-finals.

On their return to the First Division they were usually to be found in the bottom half of the table although they finished third in 1901. Nine years later they left Trent Bridge, and crossed to the north side of the river to their present ground in Meadow Lane.

One of the most entertaining sights there for twenty years was Notts County's goalkeeper, Albert Iremonger.

Albert was immensely tall, six feet six inches, very thin and dressed in a long, loose jersey. He had an enormous reach, and many a yell of 'Goal!' was stifled as Albert's long arm calmly tipped the ball over the bar.

And he did not regard his job as simply staying between the posts. In a crisis he would run to the touchline, and take a throw-in. If there was an argument in mid-field he would be there, having his say. With a character like Albert in their side Notts County were always worth watching, even though they met with little success in the League.

In the period between the two Wars Notts County spent only four seasons in Division One, once finishing ninth. It was in 1926 that their slide really began; they lost their First Division place and have never regained it since. By 1939 they were no more than a middle-of-the-table Third Division club.

In 1947–8 Notts County made a determined effort to regain their former status. They went into the transfer market in a big way, and signed Tommy Lawton, England's centre forward, from Chelsea. Lawton skippered the side, scored a lot of goals and brought on the younger players like inside forward Jackie Sewell, who later joined Sheffield Wednesday.

The result was the Championship of the Third Division (South) in 1950.

Then followed a critical period in the history of Notts County.

Their neighbours and rivals, Nottingham Forest, were also in the Second Division, having won promotion the year after the County. A desperate struggle ensued for supremacy.

Towns the size of Nottingham have not provided sufficient support for two successful clubs in recent years. One of them would have to give way.

Which one would it be?

For a time County's big buying kept their hopes alive.

Then came a shattering blow. In 1957 Nottingham Forest won promotion to the First Division. Reaction set in at Meadow Lane, and in the following year County returned to Division Three.

Their slide continued.

They were relegated to Division Four, got back after one season, and then dropped again in 1964.

What lies ahead for Notts County, the oldest club in the League? When – if ever – will there be local derbies in Nottingham like the one in 1950 when the two teams met in the promotion race from the Third Division, and fifty thousand people watched?

Today the gates have dwindled at Meadow Lane to five and six thousand. Unless more support is forthcoming soccer pioneers Notts County seemed destined to spend their time in the lower Divisions of the League, while their neighbours continue to prosper.

While County struggle in Division Four, Nottingham Forest maintain their position in the First Division. *Above:* Goalkeeper Peter Grummitt punches the ball away from a Chelsea player, while Jeff Whitefoot and skipper Bob McKinlay are on hand in case of trouble.

Soccer Scrapbook

In the poll organized by the French soccer magazine *France Football* last year to choose Europe's top player, Eusebio da Silva Ferreira of Benfica FC and Portugal was placed first. Eusebio played his first big game in the 1961 Paris Tournament, and scored a hat-trick. Since then he has been one of the outstanding footballers in the world. The leading British player in the poll was Bobby Charlton, who came fifth.

Queen's Park Rangers manager Alex Stock has signed winger Mark Lazarus four times. The first occasion was at Leyton Orient when Mr Stock was manager, and Lazarus turned professional. Then Alex Stock moved to Queen's Park Rangers, and Lazarus followed him. Subsequently the winger moved to Wolves, returned to Queen's Park Rangers, and then went to Brentford. But he must have missed Loftus Road, because last year he signed for them again, with Alex Stock looking over his shoulder once more.

Banned from football for life at the age of ten. That was the sentence given to the centre half of Featherby Junior School at Gillingham. And there was no right of appeal. What was the reason for this savage sentence? Dirty play? Bribery? No, nothing like that at all. Simply that the player concerned was a girl, and all teams that are affiliated to the Football Association through their Schools or County FA's bar women from taking part in soccer matches.

On Boxing Day 1965 four matches in the First Division were between the eight leading teams in the table. Liverpool (top) met Leeds (4th), Manchester United (3rd) met West Bromwich Albion (7th), Stoke City (8th) met Burnley (2nd), and Tottenham Hotspur (5th) met Sheffield United (6th). The odds against this happening on one day are many thousands to one. League fixture allocation is a very complicated business. Saturday fixtures are fitted first, and games involving as little travelling as possible are arranged for holidays. On this occasion the Football League could not have done it better by using any other method.

In the Fourth Qualifying Round of last season's Amateur Cup, Corinthian Casuals met Branthan Athletic, who play in the Essex and Suffolk Border League and average takings of 30s. for home matches. They put up a good fight, but were beaten 3–0.

An FA Cup-final has never been played between two teams from the Second Division of the Football League. Since the League was formed in 1888 all but five of the FA Cup-winners have been First Division clubs. The five are Notts County (1894), Wolverhampton Wanderers (1908), Barnsley (1912), West Bromwich Albion (1931) — all of them Second Division sides — and Tottenham Hotspur, who were playing in the Southern League when they won the Cup in 1901.

Memories of Wembley

Norbert Stiles

Most players have their favourite grounds — those that their team has done well on, naturally. Wembley is one of mine.

I first went on the field there as a lad of fifteen in the Schoolboys match for England against Wales in 1957. I usually played at inside forward for Manchester schoolboys, but I was at wing half that day.

Within fifteen seconds of the kick-off we were a goal up.

Our centre forward, Bobby Tambling (yes, he now plays for Chelsea) tapped the ball

inside to Brian Sullivan, who passed it to me. I made a lot of ground, returned it to Sullivan, and he pushed it out to Derek Woodley.

Derek (who later played with West Ham and Southend United) quickly flicked the ball over his shoulder, turned, and banged it into the net.

Not a single Welsh boy had touched the ball.

We had planned the move beforehand, and tried it out the previous week against Eire schoolboys, whom we beat 9–1. We did not realise it would prove so successful.

We won the game 2–0, and ever since then I have had a soft spot for Wembley. My next appearance there, however, is a bitter-sweet memory.

I joined Manchester United as soon as I left school. I had always been a United fan; nothing would drag me to Maine Road.

At first I was tried at inside forward, but found I could not make any progress. Perhaps I ran about too much without really getting anywhere. Then I went back to wing half for a spell.

I played my first League match for United against Bolton in the 1960–1 season. I made a couple of dozen appearances that year, many of them in the forward line.

In 1962–3, by which time I had become a regular member of the team, we were rather in the doldrums and our League position became really desperate. This was the year of the great freeze-up.

We were drawn against Huddersfield Town in the Third Round of the FA Cup, and the match had to be postponed twelve times because of frost, snow, ice, thaw, rain and mud. When it was finally played we won 5–0. Then we proceeded to dispose of Aston Villa, Chelsea and Coventry City to reach the Semi-finals, where we met Southampton.

I was playing at deep-lying inside forward that day — trying to create the openings. We won by a single goal, scored by Denis Law. We were there!

But we had to face a congested League programme, and in view of the danger of relegation we could not afford to take a single game easily.

In a League match against Birmingham City, I felt a muscle go in the back of my leg. No substitutes were allowed in those days; I had to play on.

We got a precious point, but I was out of action; I knew it would be touch and go to get fit for the Final.

I had a try-out against Nottingham Forest a week before the great game, but I soon realised it was hopeless. After taking part in all the Rounds I should have to be a spectator at the Final.

Well, I can't say that I enjoyed the match as much as I would have done if I'd been on the field. But it was a great experience, all the same. We beat Leicester City 3–1, David Herd getting two goals and Denis Law one. And I forgot my disappointment in all the rejoicing that followed.

Two years later we had another great Cup run to reach the Semi-finals again. We met Leeds United in Sheffield; the game was rather a brawl, and ended in a goalless draw.

The replay at Nottingham was a much better match. Two minutes from the end there was still no score; then Johnny Giles took a free kick for Leeds.

Now Johnny (who used to be with Manchester United) is my brother-in-law, and as he ran up to take the kick, I thought 'Surely one of my own family isn't going to rob me of a Cup-final appearance?'

That's just what he did.

He placed the ball accurately in the goalmouth, and Billy Bremner headed it into the net. Our lads had a few words to say about my relatives after that!

I soon had some consolation. I was picked to play for England against Scotland.

I was glad the game was going to be played at Wembley. Nearly everyone is nervous when he plays his first game for England in a full international, no matter how many times he has played for the

Nobby Stiles has happy memories of Hampden Park, too. In last season's thrilling Scotland–England match there, England were winning 4–3, but the Scots set up a dangerous attack in the last minute. With goalkeeper Gordon Banks well beaten, Nobby (No. 4), heads off the goal-line to ensure an England victory.

Under-23 team. There were two other new boys on that day — Jackie Charlton and Barry Bridges; I don't know how they felt, but playing on a ground that had been kind to me in the past gave me confidence.

We took a 2–0 lead, and then ran into injury trouble. First Ray Wilson had to go off, and, when Johnny Byrne took over his position at left back, he was injured mid-way through the second half.

Scotland scored twice to level the scores, but although we were reduced to nine fit men we managed to hold out for a draw.

Subsequently I have been lucky enough to win some more caps for England. My role in the side has been that of attacking wing half — linking up with one of the inside forwards, usually George Eastham, to form the midfield build-up for attack.

This is the opposite task to the one I perform with Manchester United. Pat Crerand does this, while my part is more defensive. We play 4–2–4 normally, and I often find myself behind the four back men, providing cover for any of them if they are drawn out of position by an opponent or if one of them moves up to take part in one of our attacking moves such as the overlap.

This line-up places a great deal of emphasis on defence, of course, but it does provide the opportunity for a quick counter-attack from deep in our own half.

I'm not very tall — just under five feet six inches — and some people think you need a big, tall chap for this job of 'Sweeper.'

It isn't true. In that position you have to be able to size up a position in an instant, tackle strongly when necessary and, above all, be really nippy off the mark. A lot of ground has to be covered in double-quick time, and the 'heavies' can't usually do that.

I enjoy the two different roles equally well, and I think it is advantageous to a team to have a player who is experienced in both of them.

Last year, in the game against Poland, we were a goal down and seemed to be making no headway against a tight defence. Bobby Moore, the England skipper, who usually plays the defensive role, went up with the attack.

I took over his position, and because of my experience of it with my club was able to perform the task without difficulty. Bobby made all the difference up in front, and scored our equaliser.

In spite of Wembley being one of my favourite grounds, I never rated my chances very high of scoring a goal there.

Yet that's just what happened in the game against West Germany last February. I was wearing the No. 9 shirt — but not really playing centre-forward because I was most of the time in mid-field. Just before half-time, however, I moved up, George Cohen crossed the ball, Roger Hunt headed it through the goalkeeper's hands, and I was there to bang the ball into the net.

It was really Roger's goal because the ball would have gone in anyway, but it was nice to see my name on the score sheet for England at Wembley all the same.

Nobby Stiles scores for England against West Germany at Wembley last season.

Play On, Ref?

Up goes a linesman's flag. A foul has been committed. Yet the offended side still have possession. The referee has to make a split-second decision. Should he allow play to go on, or blow his whistle for a free kick?

Law 5 says that the referee 'shall refrain from penalising in cases where he is satisfied that by doing so he would give an advantage to the offending team.'

Some referees seem to take very little notice of this saving clause. They blow up for everything, especially in closely-fought matches when tempers are running high. They do so because they feel that by letting fouls go unpenalised they may jeopardise their control of the game.

But if a referee ignores the advantage rule completely he is not doing his job properly. He must try to use it when he can. When he does so, he should take an early opportunity of speaking to the players concerned so that they realise he saw what went on.

When a player is fouled he may retain possession of the ball, or it may run to an unmarked colleague. The opposing defence is not in position, and an accurate pass may open up the way to goal. In such a situation it would obviously be unfair to stop the game for a free kick, and let the offending side have time to reorganize their defence.

On the other hand the player may keep possession only to be robbed in a tackle by another opponent. He will then probably appeal for the earlier foul. But he can't have it both ways; if the referee has allowed play to proceed then he can't subsequently change his mind.

Whatever he does when a player of the home side has been fouled he can expect criticism from the crowd. If he blows his whistle he'll be accused of giving a solo turn on that instrument; if he permits play to go on, doubts will be expressed regarding his eyesight. He should not allow barracking from the terraces to affect his judgement on how to administer the game according to the Laws.

A good and experienced referee will use the advantage rule when he knows he has the game firmly under control. An official knows that he can ruin a game as a spectacle by stopping it every time a foul is committed. But those watching must realize that a referee cannot weigh up the pros and cons in his own time; he must make up his mind at once. And of course he'll sometimes make a wrong decision. Usually it won't matter much — most free kicks come to nothing, anyway.

There is one occasion when it can make a lot of difference, though. A shot is going into goal, and a defender on the goal-line fists it out with his goalkeeper beaten. It only goes to another attacker, and he shoots the ball into the net. But the referee has already blown his whistle for a penalty kick.

When the kick is taken, it is blazed wide. The offended team have been robbed of a goal by a too-keen referee, and naturally they are upset. The blast on the whistle was probably spontaneous; as soon as he saw the handling, the referee blew. Could he really be expected to wait a second to see what happened next?

Spotlight on Gary Sprake

A goalkeeper must often leave his line to thwart an attack, but nothing upsets a defence more than the man who rushes out at the slightest provocation.

He is supposed to be the last line of defence, and if he gets stranded a dozen yards out his goal is wide open no matter how good the covering. In front of him interchanging of positions goes on all the time, but this fluidity is not supposed to extend to the only player in the team allowed to use his hands.

For the position of goalkeeper a club seeks a man of coolness and good judgement, one who inspires confidence every time he moves to the ball. And such a player is Gary Sprake of Leeds United and Wales.

Gary was born in Swansea, in the same street as the former Arsenal and Welsh international goalkeeper, Jack Kelsey. He came to Leeds straight from school, and made his League debut at Southampton in 1962 in rather an unusual way. He had not travelled with the side, and when on the morning of the match the regular Leeds 'keeper, Tommy Younger, was taken ill, Gary had to be flown to Southampton.

At that time Leeds were struggling near the foot of Division Two, but two years later, by which time Sprake had won a regular place in the team, they finished at the top of the table, conceding only 34 goals in League matches.

Since then the Yorkshire side have become one of the outstanding clubs in the country. In 1964–5 they lost the League Championship to Manchester United on goal average, and reached the Final of the FA Cup. At Wembley Sprake was equal to anything Liverpool could produce in the way of shots for ninety minutes, but had no chance with either of the goals that were scored in extra time to give Liverpool a 2–1 win.

When he was chosen for Wales against

An anxious moment for Gary in the match against West Ham. He is beaten by a shot, but the ball hits a post.

A great save from Alan Peacock in last season's game against England.

Scotland in November 1963 at the age of eighteen, he became the youngest goal-keeper to represent his country in a full international. Since then he has been first choice for that position for Wales.

His safe handling, intelligent anticipation and motto of 'Safety First' make Gary Sprake one of the finest goalkeepers in the country, and he seems destined to win many more international caps for his country.

And another from Chelsea's Graham in the FA Cup.

Quiz Page

1 For which European countries do the following play: Jurion, Rivera, Coluna, Metreveli, Bene? (5 points.)

2 Name the two clubs that have scored six goals in an FA Cup final. (2 points.)

3 What was the former name of Oxford United? (1 point.)

4 Players were first numbered in the FA Cup-final in 1933. How did the numbers run? (1 point.)

5 What is the highest number of points obtained by a club relegated from the First Division? (1 point.)

6 In which country was the first World Cup competition held? (1 point.)

7 Which famous Irish international became manager of Oldham Athletic last season? (1 point.)

8 Name the last Yorkshire team to win the League Championship. (1 point.)

9 In which Leagues do the following play: St Alban's City, South Liverpool, Bedford Town, King's Lynn, Altrincham? (5 points.)

10 Which England international was transferred from Arsenal to Nottingham Forest last February? (1 point.)

11 The following players have the same first name: Eastham, Cohen, Best. What is it? (1 point.)

12 Name the two League clubs that come from Derbyshire. (2 points.)

13 Which of the following clubs have never won the League Championship: Manchester City, Sheffield United, Stoke City, West Ham United, Wolves? (2 points.)

14 On which ground was the Uruguay versus France game played in the 1966 World Cup competition? (1 point.)

15 What are the colours of the shirts of the following clubs: Bradford City, Exeter City, Torquay United? (3 points.)

16 What is England's biggest win in an international match? (1 point.)

17 How many clubs are exempted until the Third Round of the FA Cup? (1 point.)

'Don't be silly, Fred. Anyone can miss a penalty.'

72

Bobby Charlton, Footballer of the Year, holding the trophy presented to him by the Football Writers' Association.

The Throstles

They called the ground The Hawthorns because years ago lots of hawthorn bushes grew in the vicinity, and flocks of throstles could be found nesting and singing there.

They nicknamed the club the Throstles — the Black Country name for a thrush — and adopted as their first crest a picture of the bird perched on a crossbar.

Today there are no hawthorns and no thrushes. The ground, situated partly in West Bromwich, partly in Birmingham and partly in Smethwick, is in the middle of a bleak, industrial area. But the Throstles are still going strong.

It was as 'West Bromwich Strollers' that they first took the field, way back in 1879. They played their first match on a patch of open ground off Walsall Street, using an inn as their dressing room. Most of the players worked in the nearby spring factory of George Salter and Co., and their funds came from sixpenny entrance fees and subscriptions of twopence a week.

Later on they used a pitch in Dartmouth Park before moving to the more spacious Four Acres, the ground of the Dartmouth club.

Soon after their formation some of the players who lived in a district of West Bromwich called Albion decided that they liked that name better than the Strollers, so they changed it.

In 1883 the club joined the Football Association and entered for the FA Cup. In those days the Cup was usually won by one of the Old Boys clubs that flourished in the South of England, but in 1882 the first provincial team to reach the Final, Blackburn Rovers, only lost to Old Etonians by a single goal.

The following year Blackburn Olympic made history by winning the trophy. In that season West Bromwich Albion went out in the Sixth Round to Blackburn Rovers, but it was not long before they made their mark in the competition.

They reached the Final in 1886, and played a goalless draw with Blackburn at the Oval. The replay was at Derby. This is the first time that the Cup was fought for and won outside London.

Blackburn led 1–0 at half-time, but the Albion kept fighting on. In one of their second-half attacks, Jimmy Brown, the Rovers' centre forward, collected a pass well inside his own half of the field, dribbled past man after man and then calmly slipped the ball between the West Bromwich posts. This gave Blackburn the Cup for the third time in succession, to equal the feat of the Wanderers.

The next year the Throstles were in the Final again. This time they were expected to beat their Midlands rivals, Aston Villa. But Villa showed their cup-fighting spirit, and won 2–0.

Undeterred by their two failures West Bromwich Albion reached the Final for the third time in 1888. This time they were the rank outsiders. They were up against the team of the year — Preston North End. Preston had defeated Aston Villa away, and in six cup-ties had scored fifty goals and conceded only two.

Two West Bromwich Albion stalwarts who will be playing for the club in the Inter-Cities Fairs Cup this season. *Left:* Skipper and Welsh international full back Graham Williams. *Right:* England international centre forward John Kaye. Their experience will be a great help to the Throstles in their first venture into a European Cup competition.

Eleven Staffordshire men earning no more than £10 per week *between them* were facing the Invincibles, a team of highly-paid players, many of them Scottish experts.

On the day the long passing and open game of West Bromwich aided by their terrific enthusiasm upset the artistry of Preston.

Jem Bayliss, a powerfully-built and free scoring centre forward, put Albion ahead in the first half from Billy Bassett's pass. After Preston had equalised, another fine pass from Bassett was converted by right winger George Woodhall.

Eighteen year old Billy Bassett, playing at inside right, made both goals. He played a great part in the future of the club, both as a player and later as Chairman.

He was less than five feet six inches in height and slightly built; yet he brought skill and craft to the game at a time when it was largely a test of strength.

After their win over Preston, Albion challenged the Scottish Cup winners, Renton, to a match for the Championship of the World. The game was played in Glasgow during a snowstorm, and Albion lost 4–1.

By this time the Throstles had moved from Four Acres to Stoney Lane, where they had their first grandstand. They had turned professional; that is, the players were paid a standard rate of ten shillings per match to make up for time lost at work.

And they had changed their colours from the original cardinal and blue quarters to the present blue and white stripes.

In the season following their first Cup triumph the Football League came into being, and West Bromwich Albion were among the original twelve members. In their first season they finished seventh, and the next, fifth. The following year they dropped to bottom. There was no Second Division yet, and having reached the Semi-finals of the Cup they were re-elected without difficulty.

In 1892 came another Cup triumph. For the second time the Villa were their Cup-final opponents – and hot favourites, since they had beaten the Throstles in both League encounters.

The Albion made rings round them.

Billy Bassett, in his natural position of outside right, was in brilliant form. He broke away down the wing with such speed and power that no Villa defender could recover in time to stop him. A perfect centre, and outside left Jasper Geddes had shot home.

Another centre from Bassett just before half-time was converted by centre forward Sam Nicholls, while in the second half a forty-yard shot from right half John Reynolds gave Albion a 3–0 victory.

Yet in the same season the Throstles were in danger of relegation to the newly-formed Second Division. In view of their Cup triumph, however, they retained their place without a vote.

They were a Cup team rather than a League team. Three years later they finished thirteenth out of the sixteen teams now in the First Division – and at the same time reached the Cup-final.

Their opponents were Aston Villa, and this time Villa had their revenge, winning by a single goal scored half a minute after the kick-off.

The Albion's League trouble continued, and in 1896 they were again bottom of the table. There was no automatic promotion and relegation yet, however, and in their 'test matches' with the leaders of the Second Division they showed their Cup form and stayed in the First Division.

At the turn of the century West Bromwich Albion moved for the last time. They went to the Hawthorns – their home for the past sixty-odd years. It had the great advantage of main road access, and was served by steam trains.

Their first Saturday game there against Aston Villa attracted a record crowd of 35,000, a very large gate for those days.

At the time a youngster named Fred

Clive Clark — West Bromwich winger, who came to them from Queen's Park Rangers for a big fee.

Everiss was working in the club's offices. Within two years, and before he was twenty, he was appointed secretary and later secretary-manager, a post he held until 1948. In his long association with the club he saw West Bromwich win every possible honour in the game.

But their first season at the Hawthorns was disastrous. Dogged by a run of injuries they finished last. This time nothing could save them from relegation.

Their first taste of Second Division soccer was brief. After losing their first home game, they were only beaten once in the next twenty-one, and finished at the top of the League.

Back in the First Division they could not reproduce that form. They were relegated again in 1904, and their financial position became serious. Attendances fell off, and they were heavily in debt. At one time the very existence of the team was in danger.

To stave off disaster the club sold their most promising players. Fred Everiss strongly disagreed with this. He felt that the strength of the Throstles must lie in the ability of the players, not cash in the bank. In 1908 a new Board of Directors, including the club's old hero Billy Bassett, was formed, and they supported Everiss's policy.

Slowly but surely Albion improved their position. They kept their best players — among them the great Jesse Pennington at left back. Pennington was slimly built for a full back in those days, but he kicked firmly and accurately, and perhaps his greatest asset was his fine positional play.

With Bob Crompton on his right and the great Sam Hardy behind him, Jesse Pennington played twenty-five times for England. He was never out of the West Bromwich side except for injury, and played for them 495 times.

Like Pennington, most of the side were local players, and their fast direct football brought them success. In 1910–11 they won promotion, and the following year met Barnsley in the Final of the FA Cup.

The result was a goalless draw, and the replay took place in Sheffield. The Albion supporters did not care for this. There was a rail strike on at the time, and many of their supporters could not get to Bramall Lane, while those from Barnsley had only to take a 14-mile journey. The result was that the majority of the 38,000 crowd were shouting for the Yorkshire club.

Again there was no score after ninety minutes. In fact there were only two minutes of extra time left when the deciding goal came. Harry Tufnell, the Barnsley inside right, dribbled the ball right through Albion's weary defence, and put a fast shot past Hubert Pearson in the Albion goal.

It was Barnsley's one and only triumph in the FA Cup.

The Throstles had some comfort in defeat; their money troubles were over. All their outstanding debts were cleared, and the club was on a sound financial footing at last. In 1912 they obtained the freehold of the Hawthorns for £5,350, and a new stand was built over the Handsworth side.

Success soon came to the Albion when soccer was resumed after the First World War. They won the League Championship in 1919–20 for the first — and, so far, the only — time.

From their 42 League games they got 60 points, nine more than their nearest rivals, Burnley.

The team cost virtually nothing in transfer fees, and goalkeeper Pearson, full backs Pennington and Joe Smith, half backs Sid Bowser and Bobby McNeal, and inside left Fred Morris were England internationals.

The Throstles did not maintain this form during the next few seasons, but in 1925 they staged another recovery and finished second in the table, two points behind Huddersfield Town. Two years later they were relegated again, and spent four seasons in the Second Division.

In the last of these they achieved a double triumph that is unique in English soccer history. They won the FA Cup and promotion to the First Division.

Their feat was all the more remarkable in view of the fact that they did not have a single easy match in the Cup. Their first tie, against Charlton Athletic, went to two replays before they won, and they beat Tottenham Hotspur, Portsmouth, Wolverhampton Wanderers and Everton to reach the Final. In every one of these games the margin of victory was only a single goal. In the Final their opponents were Birmingham.

Although half the Albion side were mere boys who had never played in an important cup-tie before the season began, they began like veterans, and their enthusiasm and team spirit swept their opponents aside. A three-man move between skipper Tommy Glidden, inside right Joe Carter and Billy Richardson ended with the centre forward opening the scoring mid-way through the first half.

Birmingham came more into the game, and thirteen minutes after the interval equalised with a goal from their centre forward, Bradford.

Scottish-born inside forward Bobby Hope made his League debut for Albion at the age of sixteen.

Before the crowd realised what was happening the ball was in the net again — at the other end.

Straight from the kick-off the Albion forwards penetrated their opponents' defence by clever dribbling and close passing. Liddell, the Birmingham right back, seemed to have stopped them, but then sent a weak pass back to goalkeeper Hibbs.

Hibbs dashed out to retrieve the situation, slipped and fell. He could only push the ball out to Billy Richardson, who scored easily.

After their Wembley victory Albion had two League games to play. Everton were already Champions. First the Throstles went to Stoke, and beat the home side by another Richardson goal.

This meant that they only had to beat Charlton at the Hawthorns to be promoted. It proved to be no easy task. Charlton put up a tremendous fight, and took the lead soon after the start.

Ted Sandford equalised rather luckily with a lob, but Charlton soon scored again, and the referee was just about to whistle for half-time when Glidden equalised for a second time with a low drive.

In the second half there was only one goal, and Richardson got it from Glidden's centre to give Albion a 3–2 win. They would still have gone up even if they had lost because their nearest rivals, Spurs, lost 1–0 to Burnley.

But they did not know that until their own game was all over, and the happy fans were swarming all over the pitch and demanding speeches from chairman Billy Bassett and skipper Tommy Glidden at the end of the finest season in the club's long history.

The Throstles spent the next seven years in Division One without really looking like winning their second League Championship, although they came fourth in 1932–3. The following year they made another appearance at Wembley — against Sheffield Wednesday.

The experienced Albion team contained nine of the successful side of four years before. Harold Pearson was in goal (he was the son of Hubert Pearson, who was Albion's goalkeeper in the 1931 and 1935 Finals); George Shaw and Bert Trentham, the full backs; Billy Richardson and Jimmy Edwards at half back; and up in front the old and tried firm of Tommy Glidden, Joe Carter, Billy (Ginger) Richardson and Ted Sandford.

But Albion were soon in trouble, and Palethorpe, the Wednesday leader, scored within two minutes.

The Albion veterans soon found their feet, but it was one of their newcomers, little Wally Boyes on the left wing, who provided the equaliser with a tremendous rising shot.

In the second half Sheffield Wednesday again took the lead, only to be pulled back when Sandford shot a fine goal from twenty yards out.

When the scores were still level with only five minutes left extra time seemed certain. Then a harmless-looking ball came bouncing down the middle towards the Albion goal. Pearson came out to gather it, but Ellis Rimmer, the Sheffield winger, got his head to it first, and it was a goal.

Almost at once he scored again to give the Yorkshire club a 4–2 win.

Losing finalists at Wembley have a habit of slumping the following season. Albion proved no exception — they finished eighteenth in the League. Yet Billy Richardson was scoring as well as ever, and he broke the club's goalscoring record by scoring 39 times.

Some of their great team were now past their best. At the end of the 1935–6 season Tommy Glidden retired, after playing 445 matches for the Albion. He will be remembered as one of the club's finest captains.

Joe Carter, his inside partner, left at the same time. Within a few years only one or two of their Cup-winning team were left, and Albion were back in the Second Division.

Their return to the First Division in 1948–9 had an element of luck about it. At one time Southampton led the table by eight points, and seemed certain to go up. Then they cracked, lost game after game, and were gradually overhauled by Fulham and West Bromwich Albion.

A draw with Albion at the Dell finally put paid to Southampton, and so the Throstles began their fifth and longest spell in Division One. In the last seventeen seasons they have rarely looked like losing their place.

1953–4 was almost as great a season for them as 1930–1 had been. At one time it seemed that it would be even more triumphant, as they were very well placed to achieve the Cup and League double.

Their new manager, Vic Buckingham, a former Spurs' half back, introduced a version of the 'hit and run' style of play that had served Spurs so well a few years before.

A typical move went something like this.

Wing half Eddie Barlow would break up an attack and put a long, accurate pass through to centre forward Ronnie Allen. Allen would move back to take it, bringing at least one defender with him out of the middle, trap the ball, turn quickly and kick it through the mid-field gap.

Inside forward Johnny Nicholls, a goal poacher in the manner of Jimmy Greaves today, would run forward as soon as the ball was played, fasten on to it and shoot for goal as soon as he was within range. And he shot well.

This sort of move brought Albion many goals. They went to the top of the League, closely followed by their neighbours, Wolverhampton Wanderers.

In the FA Cup they were equally successful. They had the good fortune to be drawn at home in every Round, beating Chelsea, Rotherham United, Newcastle United and Tottenham Hotspur.

In the Semi-finals they were drawn against Third Division Port Vale, the giant-killers of the competition, and very nearly came unstuck. Only a rather lucky goal by Jimmy Dudley and a penalty from Ronnie Allen gave them a 2–1 win and the right to go to Wembley to play Preston North End.

With the pressure on, Albion ran into a crop of injuries. To keep their hopes of the title alive they had to beat Aston Villa and Portsmouth. Both games were lost, Aston Villa thrashing them 6–1. That was the end of their Championship hopes, and they had to be satisfied with the position of runners-up, four points behind Wolverhampton Wanderers.

Vic Buckingham feared only one man in the Preston side — the great Tom Finney, Footballer of the Year. He gave the Albion skipper, Len Millard, the task of keeping him quiet.

Tom was not perfectly fit on that day, but even half-fit the Preston genius was a danger. Len Millard tackled him confidently and never gave him the chance of winning the game on his own, as he was capable of doing.

Albion scored first through Allen, but within a minute Preston were on terms and soon after the interval took the lead through centre forward Charlie Wayman.

The first goal in the 1954 Cup-final. West Bromwich outside left, George Lee, sent over a hard cross that found the Preston defence out of position. Goalkeeper Thompson failed to cut it off, and centre-forward Ronnie Allen side-footed the ball into the net.

It seemed that the Lancashire side would be able to hold on to their lead, but a quarter of an hour from the end Eddie Barlow was brought down in the penalty area.

As in the Semi-final Allen had the nerve-racking task of taking the spot kick. He made no mistake, and the scores were level again.

With three minutes to go Frank Griffin,

As Ronnie Allen takes the spot kick at the other end, the Albion goalkeeper, Jim Sanders, cannot bear to look. He looks the other way, and holds on to the goalpost for luck, keeping his fingers crossed. His prayers were answered — Allen made no mistake and the scores were level again.

the Albion right winger, bored his way in towards goal, shot from a seemingly impossible angle and saw the ball go into the net to give his side a 3–2 win.

Since 1954 the Throstles have not got as far as the Semi-finals in the FA Cup. Yet their full Cup record is impressive.

They have played in nine Finals; only Newcastle United with ten appearances can beat that. They have made fifteen appearances in the Semi-finals; only Aston Villa and Blackburn Rovers have made more. They have won the Cup four times.

According to tradition, Cup-winners do well the following season. Albion didn't — they fell to seventeenth position. But they soon recovered, and for the last ten years have been one of the most consistent teams in the First Division. Their best performances were in 1958 and 1960, when they finished fourth each time.

During this period they have had many effective players.

Bobby Robson, signed from Fulham as an inside forward in 1956, became one of the finest wing halves in the country; big Derek Kevan was perhaps the most controversial choice ever for England's centre forward but nevertheless scored a lot of goals for Albion; and two great full backs were Don Howe of England and Stuart Williams of Wales.

These players have now all left the Hawthorns, but under their new manager, Jimmy Hagan, the former England and Sheffield United player, Albion began last season in great style and were soon up among the leaders.

They had signed John Kaye, Scunthorpe's centre forward in 1963, and he developed into a fine leader. Jeff Astle, the tall Notts County forward, was the inside forward striker, and Tony Brown scored a lot of goals wearing a No. 7 shirt and wandering all over the place.

Manager Hagan put the emphasis on purposeful football aimed at getting goals by direct methods. He realised that his players

had not got a great amount of ball skill, and he gave them jobs they were equipped to do. They responded with enthusiasm, as the players of West Bromwich Albion have always done.

Stars cost money, and Albion have never been a wealthy club. They cannot afford the Denis Laws and the Joe Bakers. The majority of their great players have come to them as lads. Nevertheless if the Albion defence had been as good as the attack last year they would have put in a strong challenge for the title.

Can they ever win it again? The glittering prize of a place in the European Cup means that the giants like Manchester United and Liverpool and Tottenham will be prepared to spend and spend to take the title. And in the background the teams with the tight defences, like Leeds United and Burnley, are ready to take advantage of any slips they make.

The Throstles did, however, have a major success last season. They entered for the League Cup for the first time — and won it.

In the Final they met West Ham, and lost the first leg at Upton Park, 2–1. In the return at the Hawthorns they rattled up four goals in half an hour through Kaye, Brown, Clark and Williams, to give them a 5–3 win on aggregate.

By this victory they assured themselves a place in this season's Inter-Cities Fairs' Cup, and so for the first time the fans at the Hawthorns will have the chance of seeing some of the top European clubs playing competitive soccer there.

In the League West Bromwich Albion had to be satisfied with a place in the top half of the table, and this may be the best they can achieve with a team of triers who have not yet learned to play the clever, possessive stuff. The truth is that the Throstles are short of class players — like most of the other ninety-two Football League clubs.

The FA Cup is another matter. It is about time they made another Wembley appearance. This season perhaps?

Scottish Quiz (Total points: 25. Answers on page 128.)

1 Who was the last Scottish player to be named Footballer of the Year by the Football Writers' Association? (1 point.)

2 One of the following clubs has won the Scottish Cup: Airdrieonians, Cowdenbeath, Morton, Stirling Albion. Which one was it? (1 point.)

3 Who knocked Kilmarnock out of the European Cup last season? (1 point.)

4 For which club did Jim Baxter play before he joined Sunderland? (1 point.)

5 What are the colours of Hamilton Academicals? (1 point.)

6 Who was the last player to score a goal for Scotland against England at Wembley? (1 point.)

7 Which is the oldest football club in Scotland? (1 point.)

8 What was the former name of Motherwell FC? (1 point.)

9 Who scored Scotland's goal in the World Cup qualifying game against Italy at Hampden Park last season? (1 point.)

10 Name the only Scottish League club that has 'City' as part of its name? (1 point.)

11 Which present day player has appeared in both an FA Cup-final and a Scottish Cup-final? (1 point.)

12 Which clubs play at: Brockville Park, Tynecastle Park, Muirton Park, Pittodrie Park? (4 points.)

13 Which Scottish League club has the shortest name? (1 point.)

14 Who won the Scottish Cup last season? (1 point.)

15 For which club did Charlie Cooke play before he was transferred to Chelsea? (1 point.)

16 Which Scottish club played in the Semi-finals of the European Cup-winners' Cup last season? (1 point.)

17 Who scored for Scotland against England at Hampden Park in April? (2 points.)

18 The names of four Scottish clubs begin and end with the same letter. Which are they? (4 points.)

'After last week's game, I think I'd better start from scratch.

'This is a ball.'

GALLANT LOSERS

The young Sheffield Wednesday side put up a fine performance in last season's FA Cup-final. Here are some of their stars:

Left: Skipper Don Megson, who came to Hillsborough as a winger, was converted to a half back and is now a full back.

Bottom: A forward line of great promise.
Left to right —
Graham Pugh, John Fantham, Jimmy McCalliog, David Ford and John Quinn.

Soccer on Tour

Fred Pickering

'Off for another holiday?' asked a friend of mine, when he heard that the Everton team were going abroad.

I'm sure he thought that footballers on tour played an odd game or two, and spent most of their time sightseeing or lazing about on golden beaches. That's a long way from the truth.

A club tour abroad at the end of the season is a nice change from the cut and thrust of League soccer.

You're not fighting for two points, or battling for a place in one of the European Cups. The matches are friendlies, and you feel more relaxed than in the tense atmosphere of competition.

And you certainly get the chance of seeing new places and customs. But usually it is not more than a glimpse, and you often think how nice it would have been to stay for a couple of weeks in one city instead of being whisked off the next day in an aeroplane to play somewhere else.

Pre-season tours abroad in early August are now becoming more and more popular with top League clubs. These are no picnics. Everyone is striving to regain match fitness for the opening of the League season; they train hard, and put all they know into every game to ensure their place in the side.

Before last season began Everton made a lightning tour of Norway, playing matches in Oslo and Stavanger. I expect my friend thought we were drifting pleasantly through Norwegian Fiords when in fact we were hard at it every day. The only relaxation we had was a few hours with some Norwegian fishermen off Stavanger catching mackerel — and throwing them back in the sea.

I joined Everton from Blackburn Rovers in March 1964. I shall never forget my first game for my new club.

60,000 people crowded into Goodison Park to see the match against Nottingham Forest on a very wet day. Many of them, I knew, had come to see the 'new boy.' They wanted to find out whether their club had made a good investment.

In the first few minutes I missed an open goal.

'That's done it!' I thought. 'Now they'll let me have it.' But before they could start I'd got another chance, and I volleyed the ball into the roof of the net.

Ten minutes later I scored again from thirty yards out. That made the crowd happy. 'Wise buy,' I expect they said to one another.

It was a great feeling for me to know that I'd been accepted by the critical Merseyside fans.

Later I scored again, and we won 6–1. That's the sort of debut that a centre forward dreams about. It doesn't very often come true.

A few weeks later I had the honour of being selected to go with the FA party to South America for the series of games to celebrate the Brazilian FA's fiftieth anniversary. The tournament became known as the 'Little World Cup.'

Our first stop was in Dublin, where I watched the lads beat Eire 3–1, and then we flew across the Atlantic to New York.

I suppose every young footballer imagines

Fred *(left)* with his Everton colleague, Ray Wilson — both England internationals.

the scene when he first plays for England. The ground is Wembley, of course; the opponents — well, they used to be Scotland, but now they could be any one of a dozen countries. 100,000 crowd, lush Wembley turf, fever-pitch excitement — and so on. That was my idea, anyway.

Never did I think that I'd take the field for the first time in an England jersey in a full international a few hours after climbing the Empire State Building in New York, and in front of a mere 5000 people. That's just what happened.

And what a one-sided game! Their team would not have beaten a Fourth Division side. How the Americans beat the full might of England 1–0 in the 1950 World Cup is beyond my comprehension.

In spite of the efforts of centre-half Justo Garcia, formerly of Honduras, I managed to score three of our ten goals, while Roger Hunt got four.

From New York we flew to Rio de Janeiro.

I knew there was not much chance of my getting a place in the team for the tournament matches because Johnny Byrne was on top form, having scored three times against Portugal in Lisbon and once against Eire.

But my stay in Rio was memorable for a number of things. Firstly, seeing the city. It is a beautiful place, especially looking at it from the sea.

The entrance to the bay is less than a mile wide and lies between two headlands, the Sugar Loaf, a conical peak 1300 feet high, and the Corcovado, eight hundred feet higher.

The view from their summits is magnificent, too, especially at night when the streets are lit up with a million lights.

On top of the Corcovado is the much-photographed statue of Christ over 100 feet high. I shall never forget seeing that.

Then, in England's first game, I watched the great Pele in action. For more than an hour we held the Brazilians, and then his brilliance completely turned the game. He scored one goal and made two others, and Brazil won 5–1.

A troublesome leg injury prevented Fred from taking part in the FA Cup-final last season, but he scored four goals in earlier Rounds to enable Everton to reach Wembley.

And I saw the great Maracana Stadium, the biggest football ground in the world, which holds 200,000 people.

From Rio we travelled 250 miles south to Brazil's largest city, Sao Paulo, a modern industrial town with skyscraper buildings and incessant activity. It vividly illustrates the wealth that has come to Brazil from her main export, coffee.

The city is built on different levels, and the districts are joined by long viaducts, which allow traffic going in one direction to pass above the cross-traffic. Sao Paulo is full of these viaducts, and the most famous of them is called *Viaduto do Cha* — the Viaduct of Tea. I wonder why they did not call it Coffee?

The port of Santos, some fifty miles away, is the home of Santos FC, for whom Pele and many other Brazilian stars play.

Our match in Sao Paulo was against Portugal. Although there were several changes in the England side I was still a spectator. The match was marred by some explosive scenes following a disallowed goal by Portugal, and one of their players was sent off the field. Two others were injured, so they were virtually down to eight men.

Our forwards found the ball difficult to control on the bumpy Pacembeu pitch, and were unable to force a victory. The game ended in a 1–1 draw.

Then back to Rio for the last game against Argentina. We all wanted to finish the tour with a win, and redoubled our efforts in training. Because of this we did not see as much of the city as we would have liked, but I did manage an afternoon or two on the famous Copacabana beach.

Rio has a wonderful climate all the year round — the sides of the trams are left open to the air since it is always warm. It was winter when we were there, but quite hot enough for swimming and sunbathing — when you got the chance.

We did not get our victory, losing to Argentina 1–0 although attacking their goal for most of the ninety minutes. This made the Argentinians winners of the tournament with three victories, and without conceding a goal.

In spite of not playing in any of the games except the one in New York I had thoroughly enjoyed the tour. My only regret was that in going to South America I had missed Everton's tour of Australia, which had been going on at the same time.

I had plenty of arguments with my pals afterwards about the rival merits of Copacabana beach with the Bondi beach in Sydney.

Well, you can't go everywhere at once, and the experience I gained with the England team gave me the chance of further caps against Ireland and Belgium the following season. I was lucky enough to score a goal in each game, too.

Overseas tours are certainly strenuous, with lots of travelling and plenty of hard work, but there is a wonderful atmosphere of comradeship and plenty of fun.

I'm certainly looking forward to my next one.

'Here he comes — the team's key man.'

PICTURE QUIZ No. 2

A mid-air battle between two famous players. Who are they? One is a centre forward, and the other a centre half. Don't look up the answer yet. There is another Picture Quiz on page 106.

Spotlight on Terry Paine

Over the past six or seven years Southampton have been one of the most consistent scorers in the Football League. If they had been as successful in preventing their opponents from getting goals they would certainly have been in the First Division before this season.

During this period some fine players have appeared in their forward line — Derek Reeves, David Burnside, George Kirby, John Sydenham, George O'Brien, Jimmy Melia and Martin Chivers among them. But many fans at The Dell think that the greatest is their international outside right, Terry Paine.

As a schoolboy Terry played at inside forward, but while he was with Winchester City he was converted to a winger. He made his League debut for Southampton in 1957 before he was eighteen, and he has been a regular member of the side ever since. At that time the Saints were in Division Three; in 1959–60 they stormed back to Division Two, and scored 106 goals.

Since he first played for the Hampshire

Terry tests the Hungarian goalkeeper Jozsef Gelei with a fine shot despite the attentions of the Hungarian captain and left half Ferenc Sipos in an international at Wembley in 1965. England won 1–0, Jimmy Greaves scoring the goal from Terry's fine pass.

Wales *versus* England at Ninian Park last season. Gary Sprake dives at the feet of Terry Paine and smothers his shot. The game ended in a goalless draw.

club Paine's name has appeared regularly on the score sheet year after year. In 1963–64 he topped their list with 21 League goals; he has scored more than a hundred for them altogether.

In these days when 4–3–3 formation is so much in fashion the three strikers have to be players with finishing power. With a minimum of pure attackers it is no use having wingers who can only run fast, beat their man on the outside and put over an accurate centre.

Today's winger must be able to move back quickly and tackle hard in defence, start up an attack in mid-field, move quickly with the ball and off it, shoot powerfully, distribute the ball intelligently and be more than useful with his head. Terry Paine can do all these things – and do them well.

He received his first full international cap in the match against Czechoslovakia in Bratislava in 1963, and scored his first goal for England against the Rest of the World at Wembley later in the same year.

Then followed a brilliant performance against Ireland in partnership with Jimmy Greaves. They formed a superb right wing, Greaves scoring four goals and Paine three in England's 8–3 victory.

Since then Terry has had to fight hard to keep his place; strong challenges have come from Peter Thompson and Ian Callaghan of Liverpool, John Connelly of Manchester United and, last year, from Alan Ball of Blackpool, normally an inside forward.

In spite of being a Second Division player, great trier Terry Paine has often been in the England side in the last three years. Now he is playing First Division football at last, he'll be a very difficult man to keep out.

The goal that gave Glasgow Rangers their win over Hearts in the Scottish League Cup. Hearts left back, Chris Shevlane, makes a vain effort to stop Willie Johnston's header from soaring into the net.

Who Really Rules English Football?

Cyril Hughes

The question raised in the title of this article may seem a pointless one. Obviously most people would say the ruling body of English football is the Football Association, the oldest organization in the game, and one whose efficiency and integrity are admired and respected wherever in the world football is played.

Essentially this is true.

Over the years, despite occasional criticisms of its policies and attitudes, the Football Association can take most of the credit for superbly organizing, controlling and promoting football in this country to the status of our greatest national game, and for pioneering soccer abroad until it is now, more than any other, a 'world game'.

These are great achievements.

Yet there have been, and still are, grumbles.

The most persistent complaint is that the FA are a bunch of amateurs who should confine themselves to looking after the amateur game, leaving professional football to be controlled by the professionals.

This would mean, in effect, that amateur football would be controlled by the Football Association and professional football by the Football League, representing the most important professional clubs.

Perhaps it will eventually come to this, although I hope not.

It seems to me that it is essential to have an over-riding authority such as the FA to administer the whole of football at whatever level if standards are to be maintained, and the FA still has some strong cards to play in the struggle for power.

But if the FA is to retain the power vested in it, it must exercise it fairly and squarely at all levels. In theory it has complete authority over both individual players and clubs. In practice there are disturbing indications that things are a little different.

Where the player is concerned, the FA still reigns supreme. It can bar a player from the game for life for a serious breach of the rules. It has warned players that a referee's version of an incident will always be accepted in preference to theirs, unless the player can prove, for example, mistaken identity.

In other words, a player accused of misconduct, unlike a defendant in a court of law, is assumed to be guilty unless he can prove his innocence. And there is no appeal from an FA decision.

Very well, if not fair enough. Some people may have misgivings about some aspects of the Football Association's disciplinary procedure, but it can be reasonably argued that, if good standards of sportsmanship are to be established, it is better to err on the side of severity — and, certainly, referees deserve every possible help the rules can give them.

But let us now turn from the individual player and see what happens when the powerful professional League clubs step outside the rules.

Does the FA clamp down on them with equal severity? Apparently not.

Early in the season 1965–6 the FA circulated all League clubs instructing them to sign — as other clubs had done — the statutory declaration that no amateur players on their books were being paid. Rather than sign, the clubs, with the exception of Chelsea, resigned their membership of the FA on the advice of the Football League (though they remained affiliated through their County Associations).

What did the FA do? They gave in.

There are those who say that the whole thing was a storm in a tea-cup, and that it is high time that artificial distinctions between amateurs and professionals should be done away with, and all footballers classed simply as players, as in cricket.

I do not agree.

Football is organized quite differently from cricket. A professional footballer's wage, whether full-time or part-time, is partly a compensation for the necessary time spent in training which should enable him to achieve a standard higher than that of the amateur.

By way of compensation of a different kind, the amateur footballer has several advantages accruing from his status. He is free to practise any other sport as an amateur (whereas a professional footballer is barred from several).

He has the chance of winning a coveted FA Amateur Cup medal and other amateur honours. And he is eligible for an amateur International cap — which may considerably increase his bargaining power if he decides to turn professional.

In these circumstances, a so-called 'amateur' player who accepts undercover payment over and above legitimate expenses, or the club that makes such payments, is just as guilty of corruption as a player who deliberately 'throws' a game for money.

The fact that League clubs refused to sign the 'no payment' declaration is bound to arouse suspicion.

The very least the FA should have done was to ban 'amateur' players belonging to such clubs from all its amateur competitions and from eligibility for amateur international selection.

But these were powerfully organized clubs it was dealing with — not isolated players.

Or take another example.

Schoolboy football in this country — on the health of which the whole of the game depends — comes under the jurisdiction of the English Schools' FA. This body has always maintained that football is part of the general education of schoolboys, and that the right people to train schoolboys are schoolmasters — more and more of whom, of course, are becoming qualified FA coaches.

In particular, and with the full support of the FA, the English Schools' FA Council has set out, from 1904 to 1962, to protect schoolboys from premature pressure and possible exploitation by professional clubs.

Before the war, when the school-leaving age was 14, this was not much of a problem — clubs were rarely interested in players under that age — but the post-war raising of the leaving age to 15 meant that clubs became much more interested in schoolboy players, an interest that will be sharpened still further by the leaving age of 16 proposed for 1970.

Consequently, a good deal of touting and 'poaching' went on. The ESFA therefore had a paragraph added to an FA Rule: 'No approach of any description shall be made either directly or indirectly to a boy on the roll of a recognised school to sign registration forms or to play for a club affiliated to a County Football Association.'

Despite this, abuses continued, and in June 1962 an attempt was made at the Annual General Meeting of the FA to strengthen Rule 32(d) by an amendment (already agreed by a joint commission of the FA, the Football League and the ESFA) which read: 'No boy on the roll of a recognised school shall be signed on a form or play for a professional club.'

To the great surprise of the ESFA representatives, the League clubs, led by Bristol Rovers, opposed strengthening of the rule. Not only this, but under Football League pressure the FA rescinded the whole rule designed to protect the interests of schoolboy football!

In 1963, therefore, the ESFA was virtually forced, by what it described as this 'unfortunate decision of the Senior FA' to change its own Rule 10 so that henceforth schoolboy footballers were forbidden only to *play* for professional clubs, not to sign for or train with them.

That is the present position. Professional clubs may now train and coach schoolboys over 13 on 1 September, but boys under 15 on the same date may not play for a club.

Some people will no doubt regard it as a good thing that schoolboys should have the benefit of professional coaching and training at an early age; others, in the present context of British football, will find many arguments against the idea.

But that is not the point.

The point is that the FA retreated from a long established position, against the wishes of the English Schools' FA, under pressure from a very powerful professional organization.

The Football Association is still the ruling body of English football. Many people hope that it will always remain so.

But if it is to be worthy of its position and its power it must show that it is prepared to exercise its authority impartially, over powerful groups as well as over powerless individuals, without fear or favour.

Otherwise, the Football League may be tempted to make a 'take-over bid'.

Jimmy Greaves appeals for a penalty after a goalmouth incident in the game against Northampton Town. He gets it, and scores, to give Spurs a draw and send Northampton into Division Two.

Heads Play Their Part

In good football the ball is kept as much as possible on the ground, but inevitably it is in the air for part of the time. Then heads come into it.

Heading is often a duel for possession between two players, or a general struggle between three or four. The winner is the man who gets his head to the ball before the others.

It is not always the tallest man. Height is certainly an advantage, but only if the heading is really good. A player can beat an opponent inches taller not once, but many times.

Denis Law is not very much more than average height, yet he can out-head many taller defenders; even Bobby Collins, one of the smallest players in the game, has headed goals.

The reason is that a heading duel is not a matter of seconds but of fractions of a second, and the very tall man is unbeatable only if his jumping and timing are both perfect, as in the case of Jackie Charlton. He has turned many corner kicks into goals.

A considerable number of goals scored from close-in are from headers following centres from the wing. It is the high ball dropping over the defenders' heads that enables the man in the middle to get his chance.

The record for long-distance goalscoring

Bristol City *versus* Coventry City. Ernie Machin (Coventry) heads the ball past Charles Drury.

Ron Harris (Chelsea) jumps high to head away from George Eastham (Arsenal).

headers in a League game is believed to be held by Peter Aldis, the Aston Villa full back, who headed a goal against Sunderland from 35 yards out. Another long one came from the head of another Villa player, Frank Barson, their centre half, who headed a goal against Sheffield United from 30 yards out.

The only occasion when a player headed a goal from a penalty kick took place in 1935. Eddie Hapgood, the Arsenal full back, took the kick, Arthur Riley, the Liverpool goal-keeper, fisted the ball back, and Hapgood headed the rebound into the net.

Goals are scored by other parts of a player's body, too. The ball rolls into the net off a chest, back — even a stomach, sometimes. But you can't propel those parts of the body to meet the ball; it's only if they happen to be in the way that they do the trick.

There are people who think that there is too much heading in football, and that heads would be better employed in working out ways of providing more skilful soccer with the feet. But since the Laws say that goals can be scored so long as the ball has not been thrown, carried or propelled by hand or arm, heads will continue to be a useful part of the anatomy with which to do it.

Charlton Athletic centre forward Ron Saunders feels the impact of head against leather. Peter Dinsdale of Huddersfield grimaces in sympathy.

Quiz Page (Total points: 34. Answers on Page 128.)

1 Name the only non-League club to reach the Fourth Round of the FA Cup last season. (1 point.)

2 Who are the holders of the European Nations' Cup? (1 point.)

3 For which club did Stan Anderson play before he joined Middlesbrough as player-coach? (1 point.)

4 Only three clubs have retained their places in the First Division ever since 1946. Who are they? (3 points.)

5 What was the result of the match between England and Poland played at Goodison Park last season? (1 point.)

6 Who is the youngest player to have scored a hundred goals in League soccer? (1 point.)

7 Name the four South American countries that took part in the finals of the 1966 World Cup competition. (4 points.)

8 Who is the manager of Chelsea? (1 point.)

9 Name the two League clubs whose names begin with the letter 'G' (2 points.)

10 How many times have Sunderland won the FA Cup? (1 point.)

11 Who are the holders of the Football League Cup? (1 point.)

12 Which club now in the Southern League once played in the Third Division of the Football League? (1 point.)

13 What are the normal colours of the jerseys of the following international teams: West Germany, Portugal, France? (3 points.)

14 Name the only club that has climbed from the Fourth Division to the First Division. (1 point.)

15 For which club did Frank McLintock play before he joined Arsenal? (1 point.)

16 Of the original twelve members of the Football League in 1888, one has dropped out of League Football altogether. Which club was it? (1 point.)

17 Which League club's ground has the largest playing area? (1 point.)

18 Which teams play on the following grounds: Fratton Park, Fellows Park, Ninian Park, Selhurst Park? (4 points.)

19 Name the four Semi-finalists in last year's FA Cup competition. (4 points.)

20 Who are the holders of the European Cup Winners' Cup? (1 point.)

'So I'll get sent off five minutes from time because it's my turn for a hot bath.

99

Alan Ball — Blackpool and England.

Starting Young

Alan Ball

I've heard professional footballers say that they never kicked a ball until they were seventeen.

This may be true in a few cases, but chaps who show no interest in soccer until they reach that age and then get to the top in the game are few and far between.

By that I don't mean to say that footballers are born, not made. I believe that the most important factor in the character of a player is absolute dedication to the game, and you are more likely to achieve this if you start playing about with a ball when you are quite small.

If your father is keen on the game you may very well inherit his enthusiasm. My dad was more than keen — he was a professional footballer himself. He turned out for Birmingham, Oldham, Rochdale and Southport, and later managed Oswestry and Nantwich in the mid-Cheshire League.

Ever since I was a young lad he instilled in me a burning desire to make professional football my career, too.

From early childhood a ball was my constant companion — a rubber ball, a tennis ball, any old ball.

I remember the number of times my mother had to call me in from playing with it in the street long after dark, and with what reluctance I obeyed.

Other lads had a variety of hobbies; stamp collecting, model aeroplanes, roller skating, cycling. None of these interested me for long; I only wanted to play football, watch football, read and learn about it.

At Farnworth Grammar School I played inside forward, and when I left I joined Bolton Wanderers. After playing several games for the colts side I seemed to be making no progress at all. I was pretty disappointed — it seemed incredible that in spite of all my ambition and some ability I might have to look outside football to make my career.

When I was seventeen I spent a holiday with my parents in Blackpool. While I was there I went along to Bloomfield Road, and asked manager Ron Suart for a trial.

I played in a game with another twenty-one hopefuls, and at half time Mr Suart asked me to sign on as an apprentice. I was in.

I played a few games for the League side at the beginning of the 1962–3 season on the wing when Mandy Hill was injured, but soon went back to the reserves as inside forward.

The following year I won a regular place in the Blackpool team in the role of link forward — the job I like best.

In the open spaces in midfield I can position myself to receive the ball from a clearance, and then, either by means of a first time pass or by moving forward with the ball until the strikers in front get into position, I can start an attack on our opponents' goal.

Deep-lying forwards in the 4–2–4 system need a lot of stamina as they have an enormous amount of ground to cover. They need dribbling skill and tenacity, or they'll soon find themselves dispossessed. They need first class ball distribution, too; it's no use the other forwards running off the ball cleverly if the pass to them is clumsy or inaccurate.

And they need to be able to shoot hard for goal and use their heads with advantage when the opportunity comes their way. A link forward can find himself in a favourable position to score; when that happens he mustn't look around for somebody else who has a harder shot.

There's only one way to obtain these skills. Constant practice.

Soccer is like any other job. If you want to do well at it you must work hard. You must keep yourself in tip-top condition — physically and mentally.

It's no use being a clever ball player if you're out of breath mid-way through a game. It's no use taking up a good scoring position if, when the ball comes to you, you're too slow to seize the chance.

Every form of training must be done conscientiously. Lapping the pitch may seem boring, but it is vital for stamina; variety can be obtained by team relays — attack versus defence, or odd numbers against even.

Sprinting aids speed off the mark; the old game of 'he', in which players take it in turns to try and avoid being caught by the others, can produce unthought-of turns of speed.

This sort of training can be rather repetitive for the older and more experienced players, but modern coaches are always devising new methods to sustain everyone's interest.

As soon as the ball is brought into the training, boredom vanishes. Five-a-side practice games are both popular and instructive; on the smaller pitch every skill in the game can be demonstrated, improved and perfected. Dribbling in and out of cricket stumps, head tennis, practising restarts from free kicks, corner kicks and throw-

Alan shoots for goal with the Fulham defence beaten.

ins — every team indulges in at least two hours of this sort of training five days a week.

Most players return some afternoons to try and improve that part of their game that they think is weakest. For me that means shooting and heading.

Although the task usually allotted to me is to try and create goals for others, I'm as eager as anyone else to score them. In my first League season I was actually top scorer for Blackpool, with thirteen goals in thirty-one games. The following year I got eleven, including three in the match against Fulham at Craven Cottage.

They weren't all with blazing shots or cracking headers, but that didn't bother me. A goal is a goal when the ball goes into the net, whether it has been struck from three yards or thirty.

The first goal I ever scored for England in a full international was against Sweden in Gothenburg. In this game I was a striking inside forward — George Eastham was performing the job usually done by me with my club.

Midway through the first half a free kick from Bobby Moore was helped on by Mick Jones, and I was on the spot to stab the ball into the net. Nothing spectacular, but as thrilling to me as if it had been a thirty-yard volley.

So you'll often find me at the ground in the afternoon practising shooting from all angles, the ball being sent to me at a variety of paces and heights.

Trapping and shooting on the turn, volleying, kicking a dead ball using first one foot and then the other, I try to improve them all.

I don't suppose I'll ever be able to produce a Bobby Charlton special, but I'm going to have a darned good try.

And then heading. At five feet seven inches I can never expect to be dominating when the ball is in the air. But with practice I shall improve my timing and jumping, and in every game there are low centres coming across just asking to be converted by the little chap who uses his neck muscles properly to flick the ball wide of the goalkeeper.

Brawn counts for much less in soccer than in days gone by. Hard and tough you must be, but weight is unimportant. In fact it can be a handicap, especially on slippery pitches. I only weigh ten stones, but that doesn't bother me a scrap.

I know I've a lot to learn about this great game of soccer — and I'm determined to try and be a better player every year by practising hard and listening to advice on tactics and strategy.

One thing I'm grateful for. And that is when I was a boy a ball was my best friend. I started learning early to come to terms with this exciting, aggravating and wonderful thing.

Enjoying his training with the England international side.

Roger Hunt — Liverpool and England.

Spotlight on Roger Hunt

When Roger got his place in the Liverpool side in 1959 the Merseyside club were in the Second Division.

Although threatening to win promotion for many seasons they had just failed year after year, mainly because of lack of penetration in the front line.

Hunt changed all that. In his first season he scored 21 goals; Liverpool finished third in the table. Next year he got 15, and again Liverpool were third. More power was needed to take some of the weight off Hunt's shoulders, so Liverpool bought Ian St. John, the Scottish international centre forward, from Motherwell.

That was enough. Liverpool won promotion in 1961–2, and Roger beat the club-goalscoring record by scoring 41 League goals. First Division defences cut down his chances the following year, but he still managed to find the net 24 times.

Speed off the mark, tenacity in possession, and powerful, accurate shooting are the main characteristics of this fine example of the striking inside forward.

He was first capped for England in 1962 against Austria, and scored England's third goal in a 3–1 win.

He continued to score regularly for his club, and has played a big part in their many triumphs over the past few years. When Liverpool were League Champions in 1963 Hunt scored 31 of their 92 goals, including a hat-trick against Spurs at White Hart Lane. Not many players have ever done that.

The following year Liverpool won the FA Cup for the first time in their history, beating Leeds United 2–1 in the Final. No goals were scored in the first ninety minutes, but soon after extra time began a waist high centre came over. Roger Hunt, waiting in the goal-mouth, fell on his knees and headed the ball into the net to give Liverpool the lead, and put them on the path to victory.

In the European Cup his great stamina and love of hard work were an inspiration to his side, and they reached the Semi-finals of Europe's premier competition.

In 1965–6 Liverpool again featured prominently, winning the League Championship for the seventh time and reaching the Final of the European Cup-winners' Cup. They are certainly one of the finest teams in Britain today, and they owe a lot to the persistence of their inside right and leading scorer, Roger Hunt.

Until the beginning of last season he had made only occasional appearances in the England side. When he has played, he has often been unable to reproduce his best club form, and, unfortunately for him he has been in the side when they have given disappointing performances. However he was an automatic selection for the World Cup squad of twenty-two players.

When Alf Ramsey finally made up his mind to adopt the 4–3–3 formation there was no room in the team for an orthodox centre forward, and Roger made certain of his place as one of the three strikers by a fine display in the tour of Scandinavia.

In the competition itself, when it needed genius to find a way through packed defences, he sometimes looked short of World Cup class. Nevertheless he scored three times in England's first three games. None of his goals was spectacular and at least one had a lot of luck about it – but they were vital. On the whole Roger Hunt gave an effective display, and played a full part in England's creditable performance.

PICTURE QUIZ No. 3.

The smartly dressed fellow on the left is Portugal's top footballer; the neatly attired one on the right is one of the top referees in the country. He was in charge of last season's Cup-final. Who are they?
Don't look up the answers yet. There is another Picture Quiz on page 123.

'Penalty?'

Dennis Smith

The penalty kick is a highly unsatisfactory form of punishment. There are two major reasons for this.

One is that the punishment is too inflexible; if it is to be severe enough for a really vicious foul or a blatant case of handling the ball it must necessarily be too harsh for a mere technical offence.

And the other is that the question of intention alone makes it impossible for a referee ever to be sure — and often even to be confident — that his decision is correct.

Both faults are bad. Together they create an impossible situation which can only be resolved by referees flouting the law that empowers them to award penalty kicks.

The tendency is to give the player committing the offence the benefit of any doubt. In practice, therefore, the chances of being unfairly punished are many times less than the chances of not being fairly penalized. And, of course, the players know it.

Even when an obvious infringement by a defender has taken place in the penalty area,

What chance has a goalkeeper got of saving a penalty kick? In the Final of the League Cup between Celtic and Rangers, John Hughes takes the spot kick, Rangers goalkeeper, Billy Ritchie, dives the wrong way, and the ball is in the net.

Another penalty kick in the same match. This time Ritchie guesses correctly which side Hughes will kick, and dives that way. He gets a hand to the ball, but the force of the shot takes the ball into the net. So even when he moves the right way a goalkeeper has not much chance of saving a penalty.

a referee often allows play to continue so long as the goal is in a reasonable amount of danger and provided the offence was not vicious. In so doing he avoids the difficult decision of awarding a penalty kick.

There is another get-out.

When the foul takes place just inside the area, referees sometimes enforce a rough kind of justice by awarding a direct free kick from just *outside* the area.

They have no authority to do this; it is a flagrant contradiction of the rules. But because the law about penalty kicks is so unsatisfactory many referees take this way out.

Another way of penalising without awarding a penalty kick — also quite illegal — is punishing the offender for a lesser offence, such as obstruction, or charging an opponent when the latter was not within playing distance of the ball.

The punishment for this is an indirect free kick. It can be taken inside the penalty area, and the offending side must all be ten yards

away from the kick, but it does not often lead to a goal since the defenders form a wall barring the way to goal.

Nobody who plays or watches football regularly is likely to be taken in by these evasions of the law, but it doesn't really matter. If officials want to pretend that the law is properly enforced, who cares? A little hypocrisy is a small price to pay for the non-enforcement of a too harsh law.

At the same time it would obviously be a good thing for the game if a law could be devised that would not be evaded by those whose job it is to enforce it.

Since the Cup-final was first played at Wembley in 1923 only four penalty kicks have been awarded. All of them were successful.

Is it conceivable that in the thirty-eight Finals played there in an atmosphere of high drama and nervous tension only four offences occurred that warranted the punishment of a penalty kick according to the Laws?

Of course not! Many more have taken place — some of them much more serious than those for which the spot kicks were given. The fact is that referees have tempered justice with mercy, and have decided that it is better for doubtful offences to go unpunished than such an important match decided by a penalty kick. And morally they are absolutely right.

The penalty kick has not always been in the rules of football. It was introduced in 1892, and was an attempt to overcome the failure of a previous rule, whereby the umpire (as he was then called) was allowed to award a goal even when the ball had not crossed the line if he thought that a goal had been prevented by unethical or unlawful methods, such as hands.

Opposition to it came from amateurs, who considered it a slur on their behaviour on the field, and regarded it as applying only to the professional game. It was many years before it was universally accepted.

The law relating to penalty kicks has been changed several times, most of the changes favouring the player taking the kick.

At one time goalkeepers did not have to stand still until the ball was actually kicked — and some of them would leap up and down in the air and do all they could to put off the kicker.

Nowadays the goalkeeper has very little chance of effecting a save unless he anticipates the side the ball is coming and dives that way instantly.

So to all intents and purposes a penalty kick is the same as an award of a goal — and one resulting from a feigned trip or an unlucky bounce of the ball could be a goal unfairly obtained.

Is it any wonder then that these days a referee very often decides to wave his arms about after certain goings-on in the penalty area, instead of blowing his whistle and pointing to that ominous spot twelve yards from goal?

Another vain attempt to save a penalty kick. Peter Bonetti cannot prevent Dave Mackay's spot kick from going into the net.

Alan Peacock — Leeds United and England.

Spotlight on Alan Peacock

The north-east corner of England breeds centre forwards. They have given us George Camsell, Mickey Fenton, Jackie Milburn, Brian Clough and many others. Currently this position in the international side is causing plenty of worry to Alf Ramsey; he has tried many players there in the past couple of years, and none of them has made their place even reasonably secure. Among the ablest candidates is another from the north-east — Alan Peacock, now with Leeds United and born in Middlesbrough.

Alan went to Ayresome Park straight from school, and played for the League side when he was seventeen. He was then an inside left, forming a double spearhead with centre forward Brian Clough. In 1957–8 they scored 55 goals between them; the following season, 63. When Clough was transferred to Sunderland, Alan moved to his favourite position, centre forward. In his first full season as leader he got 24 goals in the League and 8 more in the FA Cup and League Cup.

He was included in the World Cup party for Chile in 1962 as second string to Gerry Hitchens, and gained his first cap against Argentina. He almost scored in the first few minutes, a defender handling his fine header on the goal-line; the resulting penalty was converted by Ron Flowers. Since then, like all the other contenders for centre forward, he has been in and out of the England side.

Alan Peacock is a strong, forceful leader, likely to upset any defence by his mobility and strength in the air. He is a magnificent header of the ball. Every centre forward expects to be closely marked, and has to learn to manoeuvre the ball in a small space. In this Alan Peacock excels; he has the ability to work the ball to an unmarked colleague quickly, and then to run off the ball intelligently to await the return pass.

In February 1964 he joined Leeds United at a fee of £55,000, but missed a large part of the following season through injury. He came back in time for the Sixth Round of the FA Cup, and scored two goals in his club's 3–1 win over Crystal Palace.

In the Final itself he was too closely watched by Liverpool's massive centre half and skipper, Ron Yeats, to have many opportunities to shine.

A centre forward is expected to score himself and take up so much out of the opposing defence that his colleagues can find a way through. Like the role of a fast bowler in cricket, it is in some ways a thankless task. He has to penetrate an opposing defence by speed and strength, and never give up despite all the rough handling he gets.

Is it any wonder, then, that after all the spade work he has to do in midfield and the penalty area he muffs the good chance when it comes along? Then, of course, he gets the blame. 'Good moves ruined by bad finishing,' say the cliché-ridden soccer reports.

Centre forwards like Alan Peacock, ninety-minute triers, know this criticism only too well; they take it in their stride. When the ball runs kindly for them, they're grateful; when it doesn't, they shrug their broad shoulders and try again.

A MEMBER OF THE ESCAPE CLUB

Mid-way through last season Fulham seemed booked for relegation, as they have often appeared to be in the past few years.
A fighting finish enabled them to escape yet again.

This is the man who played a great part in their revival — England international full back, George Cohen.

Right: Looking over some of the 300 footballs used in the World Cup.

Below: In a race for the ball with Grahame Rowe and Tommy Thompson of Blackpool.

That Elusive Cup

Eddie McCreadie

Everyone at Stamford Bridge really thought it would be Chelsea's FA Cup Year last season.

Among the teams we defeated to reach the Semi-finals were both the 1965 finalists, Liverpool and Leeds United. We were playing really well in the League and in the Inter-Cities Fairs Cup, although we had only survived our tussle with Milan by the toss of a coin.

The Semi-final Round of the FA Cup is full of tension. One more game to be won, and then your side is bound to participate in soccer's biggest attraction of the season. To go out at this last hurdle is perhaps the greatest disappointment a club can have.

It had happened to us the year before when Liverpool beat us 2–0 at Villa Park. Surely it couldn't be repeated on the same ground? Not against Sheffield Wednesday, a team whose League record was greatly inferior to ours?

The previous week I injured my calf muscle and ankle in a League match at Sunderland. Everyone worked hard to get me match fit, but there just wasn't enough time. Another forty-eight hours might have done the trick. On the morning of the game I looked up at the sky, and hoped for a cloud-burst. A week of incessant rain had made the pitch a quagmire; one more really good downpour would probably have meant a postponement — and then I would have been able to play.

But the game went on, and so, instead of being out there in the thick of it, I had to be a spectator, sharing every moment of hope and anxiety with our manager, Tommy Docherty.

It was a day for the big boot, and we all knew that the style of play that suited us best — close passing and running with the ball — would not pay off in conditions like that.

Bobby Tambling tested Ron Springett with a fierce shot early on, but it soon became obvious that the rugged Sheffield defence was going to be the dominant factor. Players went fearlessly for the ball; there were some crunching tackles early on, and George Graham and Vic Mobley met in a clash that left them both virtually passengers for three-quarters of the match.

The vital goal came soon after the interval. Johnny Fantham curled over a centre, David Ford headed it towards goal, the injured Mobley aimed a kick at the ball and missed, but young Graham Pugh was there to run into the net.

Chelsea fought back hard but were too often caught out of position, and I felt it would need a miracle to penetrate the strong Wednesday defence.

In fact it was Sheffield Wednesday who went further ahead. With a minute to go David Ford lobbed the ball into the goal-mouth for centre forward Jim McCalliog to head home and put the result beyond doubt.

Jim had been a Chelsea player until a few months before, and he seemed genuinely upset after the game that he had helped to knock his former club out of the competition. There is some sentiment in football, in spite of all that is said to the contrary.

Eddie McCreadie — Chelsea and Scotland.

But Jim's goal did not really matter. Chelsea were by then a beaten team.

We can count ourselves unlucky to have been beaten in the Semi-finals two years in succession. Manchester United suffered the same fate, but that was little consolation for the Stamford Bridge fans.

I came to London in the summer of 1962 from the Scottish League club, East Stirlingshire. I had been with them a couple of years, often playing centre forward although I began my career with Drumchapel Amateurs as a left back.

Scottish football is of course dominated by the two giants, Rangers and Celtic, and they share the Cup and League honours every year with monotonous regularity. Then come a few moderately successful sides, including Falkirk, whose ground is only a few miles from that of East Stirling.

Mino Scottish teams have a struggle to keep going. I remember that when I was with East Stirling the club promised us all blazers at the end of the season, but all we got were ties and badges. We were told we would have to buy the blazers ourselves if we wanted them. The money just wasn't available.

We were playing Arbroath one day, and the Chelsea manager, Tommy Docherty, had come up to watch one of their players. Later in the year he got in touch with me, and asked me whether I'd like to join Chelsea. He must have been impressed with my performance that day.

I was in two minds about coming south. I felt I needed more experience. Chelsea were in the Second Division at that time, having been relegated the previous season, but to go from the Second Division of the Scottish League to the Second Division of the Football League was a mighty big jump.

In the end I decided to go, together with my East Stirlingshire team mates Tommy Knox (now with Newcastle United) and Jimmy Mulholland, who later returned to Scotland.

I'm very glad I made the move. I went straight into Chelsea's first team at left back, and helped them to win promotion to Division One after only one season.

I must say that I find the present development in soccer fascinating. How anyone can want to return to the days of kick and rush tactics beats me. Yet you can still hear shouts of 'Get stuck in' and similar exhortations from the terraces to put brawn before brains. Hard tackling is part of the game, but not the beginning and end of it.

Some spectators have simply failed to keep up with modern thought about soccer. They still regard attack and defence as two separate functions — forwards are there to score, wing halves to fetch and carry, full backs to stick closely to opposing wingers.

That's old-fashioned thinking.

A team is most vulnerable when it is attacking. That is why nowadays there are only three players — ar at the most, four — who are classed as front men, or strikers. It is quite misleading to call players with numbers 7 to 11 on their backs, forwards. Some of them spend much of their time in mid-field, while number 4 might be the man most likely to score. Numbers are used for identifying players, not their positions.

What makes football the most attractive game in the world to watch? Attacking movements, obviously. And in spite of the perfecting of defensive formations over the past decade just as many goals are scored today as thirty years ago, when many a defence consisted of two hulking great full backs and a stopper centre half.

Why is this so?

Because so-called defenders obtain a far higher proportion of goals than ever before, and running off the ball is regarded as just as important as running with it.

The man who makes a pass and then stands still admiring it won't keep his place very long, even if his passes are invariably accurate.

Although I've played in the forward line,

A keen tackle by Eddie on Leicester City forward, John Sinclair, as the winger tries to kick the ball towards the Chelsea goal.

most of my career I've been a full back. But I wouldn't have continued to play there if my sole task had been to play a purely defensive role in the side.

Today the 'overlap' plan used by Chelsea and many other leading clubs gives a speedy back the chance of playing a full part in his team's attacking moves.

This is how it works.

With or without the ball a winger creates space between the opposing back and the touchline by wandering inside, taking his opponent with him.

His own back or half back, spotting the space created, can burst through with the ball.

If nobody moves to challenge him he can run on and shoot for goal; if he is challenged he will have drawn one of the opposing side

away from the middle. An accurate centre will then find one of his own strikers, possibly unmarked and in a good position to shoot.

I worked out ways and means of getting that move going many times as I watched the game against Sheffield Wednesday from the stand at Villa Park last April, itching to go out there and have a go.

But I'm sure my efforts would not have made any difference — they were just too good for us that day and in those heavy conditions.

Well, there's always next time, and we shall be trying harder than ever this season to win that elusive FA Cup. It's certainly overdue at Stamford Bridge, and when we next reach the Semi-finals we'll all put in a plea to avoid Villa Park.

TALENTED INSIDE FORWARDS

Above: Welsh international Phil Woosnam has a crack at goal, but colleague David Poutney gets in the way.
Below: Scottish international David Gibson skilfully evades a tackle by Eddie McCreadie.

Jackie Charlton (No. 5) and Geoff Hurst (No. 10) in a tussle for the ball during the game between West Ham and Leeds.

Their Story: Darlington

The most heartbreaking moment in the history of Darlington occurred forty years ago. They had won the Championship of the Third Division (North) in 1924–5, and were in their second season in Division Two.

They had a useful centre forward in David Brown (signed from Dundee for £80), who had scored thirty-nine goals in their promotion season; no mean feat at a time when the offside game was at its peak. They had the diminutive winger, Mark Hooper, who later won League and FA Cup medals with Sheffield Wednesday, and his brother Bill as his inside partner. And they had wing half Hugh Dickson, who made 458 appearances for the club, and sturdy defenders in Tom Greaves and Jack O'Donnell.

On the last day of the 1926–7 season Darlington were at home to Chelsea. They and Clapton Orient were level on points, and one of them would have to go down with the already doomed Bradford City.

Darlington had bright hopes of survival. They had the better goal average, and they had defeated neighbouring South Shields 8–2 a fortnight before.

Clapton Orient were away to Reading, and they won with the aid of a penalty kick. The crowd at Feethams knew that Darlington must therefore win to avoid the drop. A minute from the end they were leading 2–1, and seemed safe.

Then Chelsea broke away, and Jackie Crawford equalised. The crowd were shocked – and with reason. Darlington have never been in the Second Division since.

The club was formed in 1883, and played in the Northern League, which contained both amateur and professional clubs. In 1908 Darlington themselves turned professional, and joined the North-Eastern League. On several occasions they applied for admission to the Second Division of the Football League, but never received much support.

They played regularly in the FA Cup, however, and in 1910–11 won their way from the First Qualifying Round to reach the last sixteen.

They became one of the original members of the Third Division (North) on its formation in 1921, and apart from those two seasons in the Second Division stayed there until 1958. Three times they were forced to apply for re-election, but in 1948–9 were fourth with an excellent away record. Their average gate was more than 10,000.

In 1957–8 they were unable to get away from the bottom half of the table, and the following season were put into the newly-formed Fourth Division.

In that year, however, they had a fine FA Cup run, reaching the last sixteen once again. They won 2–0 at Rochdale, beat Boston 5–3 at home and then Norwich 2–1 away. This took them into the fourth Round, and a visit to Stamford Bridge.

Goals by Ron Harbertson, Dave Carr and Keith Morton gave the Quakers an unexpected three-goal lead, but Chelsea hit back with three goals in eighteen minutes to level the scores.

The replay at Feethams was one of the best performances in the history of the club.

After ninety minutes the score was 1–1, but in extra time Darlington scored three times to gain some revenge over the club that had sent them back to the Third Division thirty-one years before. The giant-killers got no further. In the Fifth Round they were drawn away to Wolves, and lost 6–1.

Until success came Darlington's way last season the average attendance has not been much above 4000. From time to time, however, an attractive game has been staged at Feethams, and then the crowds pour in. Just over 21,000 saw the League Cup match against Bolton Wanderers in 1960, when the home side were beaten 2–1. Another big attendance was for the Third Round FA Cup match against Arsenal in 1965. This time there was no giant-killing; Arsenal won 2–0.

Geographically Darlington could provide bigger crowds than it does. The town itself has a population of some 85,000 people, and the nearest League rivals are fifteen miles away at Middlesbrough.

But the club has to compete for support with the large number of amateur clubs in the district, including the redoubtable Bishop Auckland.

Darlington obviously cannot afford to spend much on new players. They can only exist by developing promising youngsters, and selling most of them. As soon as the word gets around that there is a likely lad kicking the ball about at Feethams the scouts arrive, and shortly afterwards the player packs his bags and says good-bye.

It is not entirely one-way traffic, though. Some established players, like Dicky Davis, Johnny Spuhler and Charlie Wayman joined Darlington from the top clubs in the north-east towards the end of their playing careers.

And last year the arrival of Bobby Cummings from Newcastle added punch to the forward line just when it needed it. A tight defence and boundless enthusiasm enabled Darlington to regain their place in Division Three.

Thirty miles away at Sunderland, First Division soccer flourishes. Winger Mike Hellawell beats Blackburn's Walter Joyce, but loses the ball to George Sharples.

Odds and Ends

'Our ball, ref,' claim all the players — even the one who knows he was the last man to kick it. This didn't happen in the early days of football. The FA rules in those days said that the first player to reach the ball after it had gone out of play had the right to throw it in. And he could throw it one-handed, two-handed — any way he liked.

When Division Three of the Football League was formed in 1920–1 it was officially called the Third Division (South). Yet one of the clubs in it was Grimsby Town — and Grimsby is further north than Liverpool. The following year the Third Division (North) was formed, and Grimsby were transferred to it. For this the club was deeply grateful — travelling expenses were cut by more than half.

Leeds United are now one of the most successful teams in the country, but twenty years ago they set up an unenviable record for First Division football. In 1946–7 they lost 30 of the 42 League matches they played. They finished last in the table, and were relegated. The worst performance of all in the League's history was Rochdale's in 1931–2; they lost 33 matches out of 40 in the Third Division (North).

A Mexican referee, officiating in his first League match, sent off six players — three from each side — in the first twenty minutes. As the game had produced very few fouls, he was asked to explain his action. 'Twenty-two players on the field are too many to control,' he replied. 'It's much easier to cope with sixteen.' He doesn't referee League matches in Mexico any more!

The record attendance for a League match in London is 82,905. That was the size of the crowd at Stamford Bridge when Chelsea met Arsenal in 1935. At that time Arsenal were League Champions, having won the title in each of the previous three seasons. Last year only 10,024 people went to Stamford Bridge for an evening game against Blackburn Rovers, the smallest crowd for ten years. The following night a mere 4,554 turned up to see Arsenal play Leeds, the lowest attendance at Highbury since the Gunners started to play there in 1913. This was partly due to the televising of the European Cup-winners' Cup Final between Liverpool and Borussia Dortmund.

John Atyeo of Bristol City retired last season after playing 597 League matches for his only professional club. He had a career aggregate of 350 goals, and never wanted to move to another club although in his younger days he was much sought-after by First Division sides. John played six times for England, the last time being in 1957, when his goal from Tom Finney's centre against the Republic of Ireland enabled England to qualify for the final stages of the 1958 World Cup in Sweden.

The first FA Cup Final was played at Kennington. Since then the match has been played at the following grounds: 1873, Lillie Bridge; 1874 to 1892, Kennington Oval; 1893, Fallowfield, Manchester; 1894, Everton; 1895 to 1914, Crystal Palace; 1915, Old Trafford, Manchester; 1920 to 1922, Stamford Bridge; 1923 onwards, Wembley.

There was a gasp from the crowd at Elland Road when the Everton team was announced for a League game last March. There were *eleven* changes from the printed programme. Everton were fielding what was virtually a reserve side, resting their star players for the Semi-final of the FA Cup against Manchester United the following Saturday. For this they were later fined £2000. Was it worth it? Well, they beat Manchester United, and went on to win the Cup.

A seven month old baby was given the following names: Paula St. John Lawrence Lawler Strong Byrne Yeats Stevenson Callaghan Hunt Milne Smith Thompson Shankly Bennett Paisley O'Sullivan. Obviously her father was a Liverpool supporter. But her mother did not think much of the idea at all. She had never been to a football match in her life.

The match between Arsenal and Valencia for the Fiesta Trophy ended in a goalless draw. So it was decided to award penalty kicks to each side, and the team that scored from more of them would be the winners. Valencia took five, and scored from them all. Arsenal's Peter Storey, Terry Neill, Peter Simpson, Ian Ure and Frank McLintock took one each — and they all scored. 5–5. Valencia took five more, and scored from four. The same five Arsenal players had another try; Ian Ure missed, the others scored. 9–9. Valencia took another three, and scored twice. Arsenal did the same; Neill missed this time. 11–11. In the last penalty kick round of two shots each Valencia scored from both, but McLintock missed his. So Valencia won this spot-kick spree 13–12, and everyone except the two goalkeepers had a great time.

Alf Ramsey, the England team manager, talks about tactics to the England players before the game against Yugoslavia at Wembley. England had an impressive 2–0 win, the goals coming from Jimmy Greaves and Bobby Charlton.

PICTURE QUIZ No. 4

Who are these goalkeepers?

Left: He plays for Sunderland, and has won Under-23 international caps.

Bottomleft: Manchester United and Irish international.

Bottom right: There should be no difficulty with this one. Leicester's 'keeper, and first choice for England.

The answers to all the Picture Quizzes are on page 128.

Northampton Town are now back in the Second Division after only one year in the top class. Many people considered they were unlucky to be relegated; they certainly played some good football. Here their right half, Derek Leck, is given a gentle push by Newcastle forward, Ron McGarry, in a duel for possession.

Football Association Cup Finals

Year	Winner	Loser	Goals
1872	The Wanderers	Royal Engineers	1–0
1873	The Wanderers	Oxford University	2–0
1874	Oxford University	Royal Engineers	2–0
1875	Royal Engineers	Old Etonians	2–0*
1876	The Wanderers	Old Etonians	3–0*
1877	The Wanderers	Oxford University	2–0 †
1878	The Wanderers	Royal Engineers	3–1
1879	Old Etonians	Clapham Rovers	1–0
1880	Clapham Rovers	Oxford University	1–0
1881	Old Carthusians	Old Etonians	3–0
1882	Old Etonians	Blackburn Rovers	1–0
1883	Blackburn Olympic	Old Etonians	2–1 †
1884	Blackburn Rovers	Queen's Pk., G'gow	2–1
1885	Blackburn Rovers	Queen's Pk., G'gow	2–0
1886	Blackburn Rovers	W. Brom. Albion	2–0*
1887	Aston Villa	W. Brom. Albion	2–0
1888	W. Brom. Albion	Preston N.E.	2–1
1889	Preston N.E.	Wolverhampton W.	3–0
1890	Blackburn Rovers	Sheffield Wed.	6–1
1891	Blackburn Rovers	Notts County	3–1
1892	W. Brom. Albion	Aston Villa	3–0
1893	Wolverhampton W.	Everton	1–0
1894	Notts County	Bolton Wanderers	4–1
1895	Aston Villa	W. Brom. Albion	1–0
1896	Sheffield Wed.	Wolverhampton W.	2–1
1897	Aston Villa	Everton	3–2
1898	Nottingham Forest	Derby County	3–1
1899	Sheffield United	Derby County	4–1
1900	Bury	Southampton	4–0
1901	Tottenham Hotspur	Sheffield United	3–1*
1902	Sheffield United	Southampton	2–1*
1903	Bury	Derby County	6–0
1904	Manchester City	Bolton Wanderers	1–0
1905	Aston Villa	Newcastle United	2–0
1906	Everton	Newcastle United	1–0
1907	Sheffield Wed.	Everton	2–1
1908	Wolverhampton W.	Newcastle United	3–1
1909	Manchester United	Bristol City	1–0
1910	Newcastle United	Barnsley	2–0*
1911	Bradford City	Newcastle United	1–0*
1912	Barnsley	W. Brom. Albion	1–0* †
1913	Aston Villa	Sunderland	1–0
1914	Burnley	Liverpool	1–0
1915	Sheffield United	Chelsea	3–0
1916 to 1919	No Competition.		

Year	Winner	Loser	Goals
1920	Aston Villa	Huddersfield Town	1–0 †
1921	Tottenham Hotspur	Wolverhampton W.	1–0
1922	Huddersfield Town	Preston N.E.	1–0
1923	Bolton Wanderers	West Ham	2–0
1924	Newcastle United	Aston Villa	2–0
1925	Sheffield United	Cardiff City	1–0
1926	Bolton Wanderers	Manchester City	1–0
1927	Cardiff City	Arsenal	1–0
1928	Blackburn Rovers	Huddersfield Town	3–1
1929	Bolton Wanderers	Portsmouth	2–0
1930	Arsenal	Huddersfield Town	2–0
1931	W. Brom. Albion	Birmingham	2–1
1932	Newcastle United	Arsenal	2–1
1933	Everton	Manchester City	3–0
1934	Manchester City	Portsmouth	2–1
1935	Sheffield Wed.	W. Brom. Albion	4–2
1936	Arsenal	Sheffield United	1–0
1937	Sunderland	Preston N.E.	3–1
1938	Preston N.E.	Huddersfield Town	1–0 †
1939	Portsmouth	Wolverhampton W.	4–1
1940 to 1945	No Competition.		
1946	Derby County	Charlton A.	4–1 †
1947	Charlton A.	Burnley	1–0 †
1948	Manchester United	Blackpool	4–2
1949	Wolverhampton W.	Leicester C.	3–1
1950	Arsenal	Liverpool	2–0
1951	Newcastle United	Blackpool	2–0
1952	Newcastle United	Arsenal	1–0
1953	Blackpool	Bolton Wanderers	4–3
1954	W. Brom. Albion	Preston N.E.	3–2
1955	Newcastle United	Manchester City	3–1
1956	Manchester City	Birmingham City	3–1
1957	Aston Villa	Manchester United	2–1
1958	Bolton Wanderers	Manchester United	2–0
1959	Nottingham Forest	Luton Town	2–1
1960	Wolverhampton W.	Blackburn Rovers	3–0
1961	Tottenham Hotspur	Leicester City	2–0
1962	Tottenham Hotspur	Burnley	3–1
1963	Manchester United	Leicester City	3–1
1964	West Ham United	Preston N.E.	3–2
1965	Liverpool	Leeds United	2–1 †
1966	Everton	Sheffield Wed.	3–2

* On replay after a draw.   † Extra time allowed.

Football League Champions

Season	Champions	Runners-up	Season	Champions	Runners-up
1888–89	Preston N. E.	Aston Villa	1924–25	Huddersfield T.	West Bromwich A.
1889–90	Preston N. E.	Everton	1925–26	Huddersfield T.	Arsenal
1890–1	Everton	Preston N. E.	1926–27	Newcastle United	Huddersfield T.
1891–2	Sunderland	Preston N. E.	1927–28	Everton	Huddersfield T.
1892–3	Sunderland	Preston N. E.	1928–29	Sheffield Wednesday	Leicester City
1893–4	Aston Villa	Sunderland	1929–30	Sheffield Wednesday	Derby County
1894–5	Sunderland	Everton	1930–31	Arsenal	Aston Villa
1895–6	Aston Villa	Derby County	1931–32	Everton	Arsenal
1896–7	Aston Villa	Sheffield United	1932–33	Arsenal	Aston Villa
1897–8	Sheffield United	Sunderland	1933–34	Arsenal	Huddersfield T.
1898–9	Aston Villa	Liverpool	1934–35	Arsenal	Sunderland
1899–1900	Aston Villa	Sheffield United	1935–36	Sunderland	Derby County
1900–1	Liverpool	Sunderland	1936–37	Manchester City	Charlton A.
1901–2	Sunderland	Everton	1937–38	Arsenal	Wolverhampton W.
1902–3	Sheffield Wed.	Aston Villa	1938–39	Everton	Wolverhampton W.
1903–4	Sheffield Wed.	Manchester City	1939–46	No Competition	
1904–5	Newcastle United	Everton	1946–47	Liverpool	Manchester United
1905–6	Liverpool	Preston N. E.	1947–48	Arsenal	Manchester United
1906–7	Newcastle United	Bristol City	1948–49	Portsmouth	Manchester United
1907–8	Manchester United	Aston Villa	1949–50	Portsmouth	Wolverhampton W.
1908–9	Newcastle United	Everton	1950–51	Tottenham H.	Manchester United
1909–10	Aston Villa	Liverpool	1951–52	Manchester United	Tottenham H.
1910–11	Manchester United	Aston Villa	1952–53	Arsenal	Preston N. E.
1911–12	Blackburn Rovers	Everton	1953–54	Wolverhampton W.	West Bromwich A.
1912–13	Sunderland	Aston Villa	1954–55	Chelsea	Wolverhampton W.
1913–14	Blackburn Rovers	Aston Villa	1955–56	Manchester United	Blackpool
1914–15	Everton	Oldham Athletic	1956–57	Manchester United	Tottenham H.
1915–16			1957–58	Wolverhampton W.	Preston N. E.
1916–17	No Competition		1958–59	Wolverhampton W.	Manchester United
1917–18			1959–60	Burnley	Wolverhampton W.
1918–19			1960–61	Tottenham H.	Sheffield Wednesday
1919–20	West Bromwich A.	Burnley	1961–62	Ipswich T.	Burnley
1920–21	Burnley	Manchester City	1962–63	Everton	Tottenham H.
1921–22	Liverpool	Tottenham H.	1963–64	Liverpool	Manchester United
1922–23	Liverpool	Sunderland	1964–65	Manchester United	Leeds United
1923–24	Huddersfield T.	Cardiff City	1965–66	Liverpool	Leeds United

Only two clubs have won the League Championship, but not the FA Cup. They are Chelsea, who played in the 1915 Final and lost 3–0 to Sheffield United, and Ipswich Town, who have never got further than the Fifth Round.

Several clubs playing in the League to-day have won the FA Cup but not the First Division Championship. They include Barnsley, Bolton Wanderers, Bradford City, Bury, Cardiff City, Charlton Athletic, Derby County, Notts County and West Ham United.

Scottish League Champions

Season	Champions	Runners-up	Season	Champions	Runners-up
1890–1	Dumbarton / Rangers		1924–25	Rangers	Airdrieonians
1891–2	Dumbarton	Celtic	1925–26	Celtic	Airdrieonians
1892–3	Celtic	Rangers	1926–27	Rangers	Motherwell
1893–4	Celtic	Hearts	1927–28	Rangers	Celtic
1894–5	Hearts	Celtic	1928–29	Rangers	Celtic
1895–6	Celtic	Rangers	1929–30	Rangers	Motherwell
1896–7	Hearts	Hibernian	1930–31	Rangers	Celtic
1897–8	Celtic	Rangers	1931–32	Motherwell	Rangers
1898–9	Rangers	Hearts	1932–33	Rangers	Motherwell
1899–1900	Rangers	Celtic	1933–34	Rangers	Motherwell
1900–1	Rangers	Celtic	1934–35	Rangers	Celtic
1901–2	Rangers	Celtic	1935–36	Celtic	Rangers
1902–3	Hibernian	Hearts	1936–37	Rangers	Aberdeen
1903–4	Third Lanark	Hearts	1937–38	Celtic	Hearts
1904–5	Celtic	Rangers	1938–39	Rangers	Celtic
1905–6	Celtic	Hearts	1939–46	No Competition	
1906–7	Celtic	Dundee	1946–47	Rangers	Hibernian
1907–8	Celtic	Falkirk	1947–48	Hibernian	Rangers
1908–9	Celtic	Dundee	1948–49	Rangers	Dundee
1909–10	Celtic	Falkirk	1949–50	Rangers	Hibernian
1910–11	Rangers	Aberdeen	1950–51	Hibernian	Rangers
1911–12	Rangers	Celtic	1951–52	Hibernian	Rangers
1912–13	Rangers	Celtic	1952–53	Rangers	Hibernian
1913–14	Celtic	Rangers	1953–54	Celtic	Hearts
1914–15	Celtic	Hearts	1954–55	Aberdeen	Celtic
1915–16	Celtic	Rangers	1955–56	Rangers	Aberdeen
1916–17	Celtic	Morton	1956–57	Rangers	Hearts
1917–18	Rangers	Celtic	1957–58	Hearts	Rangers
1918–19	Celtic	Rangers	1958–59	Rangers	Hearts
1918–19	Celtic	Rangers	1959–60	Hearts	Kilmarnock
1919–20	Rangers	Celtic	1960–61	Rangers	Kilmarnock
1920–21	Rangers	Celtic	1961–62	Dundee	Rangers
1921–22	Celtic	Rangers	1962–63	Rangers	Kilmarnock
1922–23	Rangers	Airdrieonians	1963–64	Rangers	Kilmarnock
1923–24	Rangers	Airdrieonians	1964–65	Kilmarnock	Hearts
			1965–66	Celtic	Rangers

Glasgow Rangers have achieved a number of record-breaking feats. They have won the League Championship 34 times, and the Scottish Cup 19 times. They have twice achieved the hat-trick of League Cup, League Championship and Scottish Cup — in 1948–49 and 1963–64.

Glasgow Celtic also have a most impressive record, though not quite as good as Rangers'. They have won the Championship 21 times and the Scottish Cup 18 times. They hold the record of being undefeated in 63 consecutive League matches from November 1915 to April 1917.

127

Were you Right?

Page 58 – Puzzle Page

1 Sheffield Wednesday, who were not founder members of the Football League in 1888. Norwich City, who play in yellow shirts with green collars, while the others play in white shirts. Middlesbrough, who have never won the FA Cup. Coventry City, who have never played in the First Division **2** Goodfellow, Newton, Penman, Burnside, Bloomfield, Townsend **3** Bert. The goal was scored by the centre-half **4** Hunter, centre, Graham, Barrow, scouts, Loftus, HEARTS **5** Burnley **6** Goals for, 24; against, 9

Page 72 – Quiz Page

1 Belgium, Italy, Portugal, Russia, Hungary **2** Blackburn Rovers and Bury **3** Headington United **4** From 1 to 22 **5** 38 **6** Uruguay **7** Jimmy McIlroy **8** Sheffield Wednesday **9** Isthmian, Lancashire Combination, Southern, Eastern Counties, Cheshire County **10** Joe Baker **11** George **12** Chesterfield, Derby County **13** Stoke City and West Ham United **14** White City **15** Claret and amber; red, with white collars; gold, blue sleeves and collars **16** 17–0 against Australia in 1951 **17** 44

Page 83 – Scottish Quiz

1 Bobby Collins **2** Airdrieonians **3** Real Madrid **4** Rangers **5** Red and white hooped shirts, white shorts **6** Ian St. John **7** Queen's Park **8** Wee Alpha **9** John Greig **10** Brechin City **11** Dave Mackay **12** Falkirk, Hearts, St. Johnstone, Aberdeen **13** Clyde **14** Rangers **15** Dundee **16** Celtic **17** Denis Law, Jimmy Johnstone (2) **18** Celtic, Dundee United, Kilmarnock, East Fife

Page 99 – Quiz Page

1 Bedford Town **2** Spain **3** Newcastle United **4** Arsenal, Blackpool, Manchester United **5** A draw, 1–1 **5** Jimmy Greaves **7** Argentina, Brazil, Uruguay, Chile **8** Tommy Docherty **9** Gillingham, Grimsby Town **10** Once **11** West Bromwich Albion **12** Merthyr Tydvil **13** White, red, blue **14** Northampton Town **15** Leicester City **16** Accrington Stanley **17** Doncaster Rovers **18** Portsmouth, Walsall, Cardiff City, Crystal Palace **19** Chelsea, Everton, Manchester United, Sheffield Wednesday **20** Borussia Dortmund

Picture Quiz

Page 49: (top) Mike Bailey; (bottom left) Alex Dawson; (bottom right) Charlie Hurley
Page 89: Ian St John of Liverpool (left) and Billy Foulkes of Manchester United
Page 106: Eusebio of Benfica and Portugal (left); Jack Taylor (right).
Page 123: (top) Jimmy Montgomery; (bottom left) Harry Gregg; (bottom right) Gordon Banks

Acknowledgements

Photographs reproduced by permission of Syndication International, P.A.-Reuter and Beaverbrook Newspapers Ltd. Cartoons by Rich.

WHERE THEY PLAY — WHAT THEY WEAR

BELOW are the names of 129 League clubs (including Scottish) with their home grounds and colours.

It is an accepted rule that when two teams with the same colours are playing each other, the visiting team must make a temporary change.

Under the laws of the game a goalkeeper is not allowed to wear the same colours as the rest of the team.

ENGLAND AND WALES

Accrington Stanley : Peel Park, Accrington ; red shirts, white collars and sleeves, white shorts.

Aldershot : Recreation Ground, Aldershot ; red shirts, blue sleeves, white shorts.

Arsenal : Arsenal Stadium, London, N.5 ; red shirts, white sleeves and collars, white shorts.

Aston Villa : Villa Park, Birmingham 6 ; claret shirts, blue sleeves and collars, white shorts.

Barnsley : Oakwell, Barnsley ; red shirts, white shorts.

Barrow : Holker Street, Barrow-in-Furness ; blue shirts, white shorts.

Birmingham City : St. Andrew's, Birmingham 9 ; blue shirts, white collars and cuffs, white shorts.

Blackburn Rovers : Ewood Park, Blackburn ; blue and white halves, white shorts.

Blackpool : Bloomfield Road, Blackpool ; tangerine shirts, white collars and cuffs, white shorts.

Bolton Wanderers : Burnden Park, Bolton ; white shirts, blue shorts.

Bournemouth and Boscombe : Dean Court, Bournemouth ; red shirts, white sleeves and collars, white shorts.

Bradford (P.A.) : Park Avenue, Bradford ; green and white stripes, white shorts with green seam.

Bradford City : Valley Parade, Bradford ; claret shirts, amber collars and cuffs, white shorts.

Brentford : Griffin Park, Brentford ; red and white stripes, black shorts.

Brighton and Hove Albion : Goldstone Ground, Hove ; blue and white stripes, white shorts.

Bristol City : Ashton Gate, Bristol 3 ; red shirts, white sleeves and collars, white shorts.

Bristol Rovers : Eastville Stadium, Bristol 5 ; blue and white quarters, white shorts.

Burnley : Turf Moor, Burnley ; claret shirts, blue sleeves and collars, white shorts.

Bury : Gigg Lane, Bury ; white shirts, blue shorts with white seam.

Cardiff City : Ninian Park, Cardiff ; blue shirts, white collars, white shorts.

Carlisle United : Brunton Park, Carlisle ; blue shirts, white shorts.

Charlton Athletic : The Valley, Charlton, London, S.E.7 ; red shirts, white collars, white shorts.

Chelsea ; Stamford Bridge, London, S.W.6 ; blue shirts, white collars, white shorts.

Chester : Sealand Road Stadium, Chester ; blue and white stripes, black shorts.

Chesterfield : Saltergate, Chesterfield ; blue shirts, white shorts.

Colchester United : Layer Road, Colchester ; blue and white stripes, white shorts.

Coventry City : Highfield Road, Coventry ; blue and white halves, white shorts.

Crewe Alexandra : Gresty Road, Crewe ; scarlet shirts, white shorts.

Crystal Palace : Selhurst Park, South Norwood, London, S.E.25 ; white shirts, claret and blue collars, black shorts.

Darlington : Feethams Ground, Darlington ; white shirts, black shorts.

Derby County : Baseball Ground, Derby ; white shirts, black shorts.

Doncaster Rovers : Belle Vue, Doncaster ; red shirts, white shorts with red stripe.

Everton : Goodison Park, Liverpool 4 ; blue shirts, white shorts with blue stripe.

Exeter City : St. James's Park, Exeter ; red shirts, white collars, white shorts.

Fulham : Craven Cottage, London, S.W.6 ; white shirts, black shorts.

Gateshead : Redheugh Park, Gateshead ; white shirts, black shorts.

Gillingham : Priestfield Stadium, Gillingham ; blue shirts, white collars and cuffs, white shorts.

Grimsby Town : Blundell Park, Cleethorpes ; black and white stripes, black shorts.

Halifax Town : Shay Ground, Halifax ; blue shirts, white collars and cuffs, white shorts with blue stripe.

Hartlepools United : Victoria Ground, West Hartlepool ; blue and white halves, black shorts.

Huddersfield Town : Leeds Road, Huddersfield ; blue and white stripes, white shorts.

Hull City : Boothferry Park, Hull ; amber shirts, black collars, black shorts.

Ipswich Town : Portman Road, Ipswich ; blue shirts, white sleeves and collars, white shorts.

Leeds United : Elland Road, Leeds 11 ; blue shirts, old gold collars, white shorts.

Leicester City : Filbert Street, Leicester ; blue shirts, white collars and cuffs, white shorts with blue stripe.

Leyton Orient : Brisbane Road, London, E.10 ; blue shirts, white collars, white shorts.

Lincoln City : Sincil Bank, Lincoln ; red and white stripes, black shorts.

Liverpool : Anfield Road, Liverpool 4 ; red shirts, white collars, white shorts.

Luton Town : Kenilworth Road, Luton ; white shirts, black shorts.

Manchester City : Maine Road, Moss Side, Manchester 14 ; sky-blue shirts, white collars, white shorts.

Manchester United : Old Trafford, Manchester 16 ; red shirts, white collars, white shorts.

Mansfield Town : Field Mill, Mansfield ; white shirts, black shorts.

Middlesbrough : Ayresome Park, Linthorpe, Middlesbrough ; red shirts, white collars and cuffs, white shorts.

Millwall : The Den, New Cross, London, S.E.14 ; blue shirts, white collars and cuffs, white shorts with blue stripe.

Newcastle United : St. James's Park, Newcastle ; black and white stripes, black shorts.

Newport County : Somerton Park, Newport ; amber shirts, black collars and cuffs, black shorts with amber stripe.

Northampton Town : County Ground, Northampton ; claret shirts, white collars and cuffs, white shorts.

Norwich City : Carrow Road, Norwich ; yellow shirts, green collars and cuffs, black shorts with yellow stripe.

Nottingham Forest : City Ground, Nottingham ; red shirts, white shorts.

Notts County : Meadow Lane, Nottingham ; white shirts with black collars, black shorts.

Oldham Athletic : Boundary Park, Oldham ; blue and white stripes, white shorts.

Plymouth Argyle : Home Park, Plymouth ; green shirts, white collars and cuffs, white shorts.

Port Vale : Vale Park, Burslem ; black and white stripes, black shorts.

Portsmouth : Fratton Park, Portsmouth ; blue shirts, white shorts.

Preston North End : Deepdale, Preston ; white shirts, dark blue shorts.

Queen's Park Rangers : Loftus Road, Shepherd's Bush, London, W.12 ; white shirts, blue collars and cuffs, blue shorts.

Reading : Elm Park, Reading ; blue and white hoops, white shorts.

Rochdale : Spotland, Rochdale ; royal blue shirts, white collars and cuffs, white shorts.

Rotherham United : Millmoor Ground, Rotherham ; red shirts, white collars and sleeves, white shorts.

Scunthorpe and Lindsey United : Old Show Ground, Scunthorpe ; claret shirts, blue sleeves and collars, white shorts.

Sheffield United : Bramall Lane, Sheffield 2 ; red and white stripes, black shorts.

Sheffield Wednesday : Hillsborough, Sheffield 6 ; blue and white stripes, dark-blue shorts.

Shrewsbury Town : Gay Meadow, Shrewsbury ; blue shirts, white collars and cuffs, white shorts.

Southampton : The Dell, Milton Road, Southampton ; red and white stripes, black shorts.

Southend United : Roots Hall, Southend ; blue shirts, white collars and cuffs, white shorts.

Southport : Haig Avenue, Southport ; black and white stripes, black shorts.

Stockport County : Edgeley Park, Stockport ; white shirts, black shorts.

Stoke City : Victoria Ground, Stoke-on-Trent ; red and white stripes, white shorts.

Sunderland : Roker Park, Sunderland ; red and white stripes, black shorts.

Swansea Town : Vetch Field, Swansea ; white shirts, white shorts.

Swindon Town : County Ground, Swindon ; red shirts, white collars, white shorts.

Torquay United : Plainmoor Ground, Torquay ; old gold shirts, blue sleeves and collars, black shorts.

Tottenham Hotspur : White Hart Lane, Tottenham, London, N.17 ; white shirts, blue shorts.

Tranmere Rovers : Prenton Park, Birkenhead ; blue shirts, white shorts with blue stripe.

Walsall : Fellows Park, Walsall ; red shirts, white collars, white shorts.

Watford : Vicarage Road Ground, Watford ; blue shirts, white collars and cuffs, white shorts.

West Bromwich Albion : The Hawthorns, West Bromwich ; blue and white stripes, white shorts.

West Ham United : Upton Park, London, E.13 ; claret shirts, blue sleeves and collars, white shorts.

Wolverhampton Wanderers : Molineux Grounds, Wolverhampton ; old gold shirts, black collars, black shorts.

Workington Town : Borough Park, Workington ; red shirts, white shorts.

Wrexham : Racecourse Ground, Wrexham ; red shirts, white collars and cuffs, white shorts with red stripe.

York City : Bootham Crescent, York ; red shirts, white collars, white shorts.

SCOTLAND

Aberdeen : Pittodrie Park, Aberdeen ; red shirts, white collars, white shorts.

Airdrieonians : Broomfield Park, Airdrie ; white shirts with red diamond, white shorts.

Albion Rovers : Cliftonhill Park, Coatbridge ; royal blue shirts, white shorts.

Alloa : Recreation Ground, Alloa ; orange and black hoops, white shorts.

Arbroath : Gayfield Park, Arbroath ; maroon shirts, white shorts.

Ayr United : Somerset Park, Ayr ; white shirts, black shorts.

Berwick Rangers : Shielfield Park, Tweedmouth, Berwick-on-Tweed ; black and gold.

Brechin City : Glebe Park, Brechin ; scarlet shirts, white shorts.

Celtic : Celtic Park, Glasgow ; green and white hoops, white shorts.

Clyde : Shawfield Park, Glasgow ; red shirts, white collars, white shorts.

Cowdenbeath : Central Park, Cowdenbeath ; royal blue shirts, white shorts.

Dumbarton : Boghead Park, Dumbarton ; black and gold shirts, white knickers.

Dundee : Dens Park, Dundee ; navy blue shirts, white shorts.

Dundee United : Tannadice Park, Dundee ; black and white hoops, white shorts.

Dunfermline Athletic : East End Park, Dunfermline ; black and white stripes, white shorts.

East Fife : Bayview Park, Methil ; black and gold stripes, white shorts.

East Stirling : Firs Park ; black and white.

Falkirk : Brockville Park, Falkirk ; blue shirts, red sleeves, white shorts.

Forfar Athletic : Station Park, Forfar ; green shirts, white shorts.

Hamilton Academicals : Douglas Park, Hamilton ; red and white hoops, white shorts.

Heart of Midlothian : Tynecastle Park, Edinburgh 11; maroon shirts, white collars, white shorts.

Hibernian : Easter Road Park, Edinburgh ; green shirts, white sleeves, white shorts.

Kilmarnock : Rugby Park, Kilmarnock ; light blue and white hoops, white shorts.

Montrose : Links Park, Montrose ; royal blue and white hoops, white shorts.

Morton : Cappielow Park, Greenock ; blue and white hoops, white shorts.

Motherwell : Fir Park, Motherwell ; claret and amber bands, white shorts.

Partick Thistle : Firhill Park, Glasgow ; red and yellow hoops, white shorts.

Queen of the South : Palmerston Park, Dumfries ; royal blue shirts, white shorts.

Queen's Park : Hampden Park, Glasgow ; black and white hoops, white shorts.

Raith Rovers : Starks Park, Kirkcaldy ; navy blue shirts, white shorts.

Rangers : Ibrox Park, Glasgow ; royal blue shirts, white shorts.

St. Johnstone : Muirton Park, Perth ; royal blue shirts, white collars and cuffs, white shorts.

St. Mirren : St. Mirren Park, Paisley ; black and white stripes, black shorts.

Stenhousemuir : Ochilview Park, Stenhousemuir ; maroon shirts, white shorts.

Stirling Albion : Annfield Park, Stirling ; red shirts, white shorts.

Stranraer : Stair Park, Stranraer ; royal blue.

Third Lanark : Cathkin Park, Glasgow ; scarlet shirts, white shorts.

The Laws of the Game

Note.—Provided the principles of these Laws be maintained they may be modified in their application to players of school age, as follows : (*a*) size of playing pitch ; (*b*) size and weight of ball ; (*c*) width between the goal-posts and height of the cross-bar from the ground ; (*d*) the duration of the periods of play.

I.—THE FIELD OF PLAY

The field of play and appurtenances shall be as shown in the plan below:

1. Dimensions. The field of play shall be rectangular, its length being not more than 130 yards nor less than 100 yards and its breadth not more than 100 yards nor less than 50 yards. (In International Matches the length shall be not more than 120 yards nor less than 110 yards and the breadth not more than 80 yards nor less than 70 yards.) The length shall in all cases exceed the breadth.

2. Marking. The field of play shall be marked with distinctive lines, not more than 5 inches in width, not by a V-shaped rut, in accordance with the plan, the longer boundary lines being called the touch lines and the shorter the goal-lines. A flag on a post not less than 5 feet high, and having a non-pointed top, shall be placed at each corner ; a similar flag-post may be placed opposite the half-way line on each side of the field of play, not less than one yard outside the touch-line. A half-way line shall be marked out across the field of play. The centre of the field of play shall be indicated by a suitable mark and a circle with a 10-yards radius shall be marked round it.

3. The Goal Area. At each end of field of play two lines shall be drawn at right angles to the goal-line, 6 yards from each goal-post. These shall extend into the field of play for a distance of 6 yards and shall be joined by a line drawn parallel with the goal-line. Each of the spaces enclosed by these lines and the goal-line shall be called a goal area.

4. The Penalty Area. At each end of the field of play two lines shall be drawn at right angles to the goal-line, 18 yards from each goal-post. These shall extend into the field of play for a distance of 18 yards and shall be joined by a line drawn parallel with the goal-line. Each of the spaces enclosed by these lines and the goal-line shall be called a penalty area. A suitable mark shall be made within each penalty area, 12 yards from the mid-point of the goal-line, measured along an undrawn line at right angles thereto. These shall be the penalty-kick marks. From each penalty-kick mark an arc of a circle, having a radius of 10 yards, shall be drawn outside the penalty area.

5. Corner Area. From each corner-flag post a quarter circle, having a radius of 1 yard, shall be drawn inside the field of play.

6. The Goals. The goals shall be placed

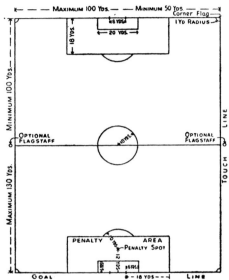

on the centre of each goal-line and shall consist of two upright posts equidistant from the corner-flags and 8 yards apart (inside measurement), joined by a horizontal cross-bar, the lower edge of which shall be 8 feet from the ground. The width and depth of the goal-posts and the width and depth of the cross-bars shall not exceed 5 inches.

Nets may be attached to the posts, cross-bars, and ground behind the goals. They should be appropriately supported and be so placed as to allow the goalkeeper ample room.

II.—THE BALL

The ball shall be spherical ; the outer casing shall be of leather, and no material shall be used in its construction which might prove dangerous to the players. The circumference of the ball shall not be more than 28 inches nor less than 27 inches. The weight of the ball at the start of the game shall not be more than 16 ounces nor less than 14 ounces, and it shall not be changed during the game unless authorised by the Referee.

III.—NUMBER OF PLAYERS

1. The game shall be played by two teams, each consisting of not more than eleven players, one of whom shall be the goalkeeper. One of the other players may change places with the goalkeeper during the match provided notice be given to the Referee before such change is made.

2. Substitutes for players injured during a match played under the Rules of a Competition will only be permitted if the approval

of the National Association or International Association concerned has been obtained.

3. Substitutes for injured players may be introduced in other matches subject to this arrangement being agreed upon by both teams before the start of a match.

Punishment. If, without notifying the Referee, a player changes to goalkeeper during the game, and then handles the ball within the penalty area, a penalty kick shall be awarded. Any player leaving the field during the progress of the game (except through accident) without the consent of the Referee shall be deemed guilty of ungentlemanly conduct.

IV.—PLAYERS' EQUIPMENT

A player shall not wear anything which is dangerous to another player. Boots must conform to the following standard :

(*a*) Bars and studs must be made of leather, soft rubber, aluminium, plastic, or similar material; if nails are used they shall be driven in flush with the surface.

(*b*) Bars shall be transverse and flat, not less than half an inch in width and they shall extend the total width of the boot and be rounded at the corners.

(*c*) Studs shall be round in plan and not less than half an inch in diameter. Where studs are tapered the minimum diameter of any section of a stud must not be less than half an inch. Where metal seating for the screw type is used, this seating must be embedded in the sole of the boot and any attachment screw shall be part of the stud. Other than the metal seating for the screw type of stud, no metal plates, even though covered with leather or rubber shall be worn; neither studs which are threaded to allow them to be screwed on to a base screw that is fixed by nails or otherwise to the soles of boots, nor studs with any form of protruding edge, rim or relief marking or ornament shall be allowed.

(*d*) Combined bars and studs may be worn, provided the whole conforms to the general requirements of this law; neither bars nor studs on the soles or heels shall project more than three quarters of an inch.

N.B.—The usual equipment of a player consists of a jersey or shirt, shorts, stockings, and boots. A goalkeeper shall wear colours which distinguish him from the other players.

Punishment. For any infringement of this Law, the player at fault shall be sent off the field of play to adjust his equipment, and he shall not return without first reporting to the Referee, who shall satisfy himself that the player's equipment is in order; the player shall only re-enter the game at a moment when the ball has ceased to be in play.

V.—REFEREES

A Referee shall be appointed to officiate in each game. He shall :

(*a*) Enforce the Laws and decide any disputed point. His decision on points of fact connected with the play shall be final so far as the result of the game is concerned. His jurisdiction begins from the time he signals for the kick-off, and his power of penalising shall extend to offences committed when play has been temporarily suspended or when the ball is out of play. He shall, however, refrain from penalising in cases where he is satisfied that by doing so he would be giving an advantage to the offending team.

(b) Keep a record of the game ; act as timekeeper and allow the full or agreed time, adding thereto all time lost through accident or other cause.

(c) Have discretionary power to stop the game for any infringement of the Laws and to suspend or terminate the game whenever, by reason of the elements, interference by spectators, or other cause, he deems such stoppage necessary. In such a case he shall report the matter to the National or Affiliated Association under whose jurisdiction the game was played within two days (Sundays not included). Reports will be deemed to be made when received in the ordinary course of post.

(d) Have discretionary power, from the time he enters the field of play, to caution any player guilty of misconduct or ungentlemanly behaviour, and if he persists, to suspend him from further participation in the game. In such cases the Referee shall send the name of the offender to the National or Affiliated Association concerned within two days after the occurrence (Sundays not included). Reports will be deemed to be made when received in the ordinary course of post.

(e) Allow no person other than the players and Linesmen to enter the field of play without his permission.

(f) Stop the game, if in his opinion a player has been seriously injured ; have the player removed as soon as possible from the field of play and immediately resume the game. If a player is slightly injured, the game shall not be stopped until the ball has ceased to be in play. A player who is able to go to the touch- or goal-line for attention of any kind shall not be treated on the field of play.

Have discretionary power to suspend from further participation in the game, without previous caution, a player guilty of violent conduct.

(h) Signal for recommencement of the game after all stoppages.

(i) Decide that the ball provided for a match meets with the requirements of Law 2.

VI.—LINESMEN

Two Linesmen shall be appointed whose duty (subject to the decision of the Referee) shall be to indicate when the ball is out of play and which side is entitled to the corner kick, goal kick, or throw-in. They shall also assist the Referee to control the game in accordance with the Laws. In the event of undue interference or improper conduct by a Linesman, the Referee shall dispense with his services and arrange for a substitute to be appointed. (The matter shall be reported by the Referee to the National or Affiliated Association having jurisdiction over the offending Linesman.) The Linesmen should be equipped with flags by the club on whose ground the match is played.

VII.—DURATION OF THE GAME

The duration of the game shall be two equal periods of 45 minutes, unless otherwise mutually agreed upon, subject to the following : (a) allowance shall be made in either period for all time lost through accident or other cause, the amount of which shall be a matter for the discretion of the Referee ; (b) time shall be extended to permit of a penalty kick being taken at or after the expiration of the normal period in either half.

At half-time the interval shall not exceed five minutes except by the consent of the Referee.

VIII.—THE START OF THE PLAY

(a) **At the beginning of the game :** choice of ends and the kick-off shall be decided by the toss of a coin. The team winning the toss shall have the option of choice of ends or the kick-off.

The Referee having given a signal, the game shall be started by a player taking a place-kick (i.e., a kick at the ball while it is stationary on the ground in the centre of the field of play) into his opponents' half of the field of play. Every player shall be in his own half of the field and every player of the team opposing that of the kicker shall remain not less than 10 yards from the ball until it is kicked-off ; it shall not be deemed in play until it has travelled the distance of its own circumference. The kicker shall not play the ball a second time until it has been played or touched by another player.

(b) **After a goal has been scored :** the game shall be restarted in like manner by a player of the team losing the goal.

(c) **After half-time :** when restarting after half-time, ends shall be changed and the kick-off shall be taken by a player of the opposite team to that of the player who started the game.

Punishment. For any infringement of this Law the kick-off shall be retaken, except in the case of the kicker playing the ball again before it has been touched or played by another player ; for this offence an indirect free kick shall be taken by a player of the opposing team from the place where the infringement occurred. A goal shall not be scored direct from a kick-off.

(d) **After any other temporary suspension :** when restarting the game after a temporary suspension of play from any cause not mentioned elsewhere in these Laws, provided that immediately prior to the suspension the ball has not passed over the touch- or goal-lines, the Referee shall drop the ball at the place where it was when play was suspended and it shall be deemed in play when it has touched the ground ; if, however, it goes over the touch- or goal-lines after it has been dropped by the Referee, but before it is touched by a player, the Referee shall again drop it. A player shall not play the ball until it has touched the ground. If this section of the Law is not complied with the Referee shall again drop the ball.

IX.—BALL IN AND OUT OF PLAY

The ball is out of play :

(a) When it has wholly crossed the goal-line or touch-line whether on the ground or in the air.

(b) When the game has been stopped by the Referee.

The ball is in play at all other times from the start of the match to the finish, including :

(a) If it rebounds from a goal-post, cross-bar, or corner-flag post into the field of play.

(b) If it rebound off either the Referee or Linesmen when they are in the field of play.

(c) In the event of a supposed infringement of the Laws until a decision is given.

X.—METHOD OF SCORING

Except as otherwise provided by these Laws, a goal is scored when the whole of the ball has passed over the goal-line, between the goal-posts and under the cross-bar, provided it has not been thrown, carried or propelled by hand or arm by a player of the attacking side. Should the cross-bar become displaced, for any reason during the game, and the ball cross the goal-line at a point which, in the opinion of the Referee, is below where the cross-bar should have been, he shall award a goal.

The team scoring the greater number of goals during a game shall be the winner ; if no goals or an equal number of goals are scored the game shall be termed a " draw."

XI.—OFF-SIDE

A player is off-side if he is nearer his opponents' goal-line than the ball **at the moment the ball is played unless :**

(a) He is in his own half of the field of play.

(b) There are two of his opponents nearer to their own goal-line than he is.

(c) The ball last touched an opponent or was last played by him.

(d) He receives the ball direct from a goal kick, a corner kick, a throw-in, or when it is dropped by the Referee.

Punishment. For an infringement of this Law an indirect free kick shall be taken by a player of the opposing team from the place where the infringement occurred.

A player in an off-side position shall not be penalised unless, in the opinion of the Referee, he is interfering with the play or with an opponent, or is seeking to gain an advantage by being in an off-side position.

XII.—FOULS AND MISCONDUCT

1. A player who intentionally commits any of the following nine offences :

(a) Kicks or attempts to kick an opponent;

(b) Trips an opponent, i.e., throwing or attempting to throw him by the use of the legs or by stooping in front of or behind him;

(c) Jumps at an opponent;

(d) Charges an opponent in a violent or dangerous manner;

(e) Charges an opponent from behind unless the latter be obstructing;

(f) Strikes or attempts to strike an opponent ;

(g) Holds an opponent with the hand or any part of his arm ;

(h) Pushes an opponent with his hand or any part of his arm ;

(i) Handles the ball, i.e., carries, strikes or propels the ball with his hand or arm. (This does not apply to the goalkeeper within his own penalty area) ;

shall be penalised by the award of a **direct free kick** to be taken by the opposing side from the place where the offence occurred.

Should a player of the defending side intentionally commit one of the above nine offences **within the penalty area** he shall be penalised by a **penalty kick**.

A penalty kick can be awarded irrespective of the position of the ball, if in play, at the time an offence within the penalty area is committed.

2. A player committing any of the five following offences :

(1) Playing in a manner considered by the Referee to be dangerous, *e.g.*, attempting to kick the ball while held by the goalkeeper;

(2) Charging fairly, *i.e.*, with the shoulder, when the ball is not within playing distance of the players concerned and they are definitely not trying to play it;

(3) When not playing the ball, intentionally obstructing an opponent, *i.e.*, running between the opponent and the ball, or interposing the body so as to form an obstacle to an opponent;

(4) Charging the goalkeeper except when he—

(a) is holding the ball;
(b) is obstructing an opponent;
(c) has passed outside his goal area;

(5) When playing as goalkeeper, carrying the ball, *i.e.*, taking more than four steps while holding the ball without bouncing it on the ground;

shall be penalised by the award of an **indirect free kick** to be taken by the opposing side from the place where the infringement occurred.

3. A player shall be **cautioned** if

(j) He enters the field of play to join or rejoin his team after the game has commenced without first having received a signal from the Referee showing him that he is in order to do so. (This clause is not applicable in the case of Law 4.) If the game has been stopped (to administer the caution) it shall be restarted by the Referee dropping the ball at the place where the infringement occurred, but if the player has committed a more important offence he shall be penalised according to that section of the Law infringed.

(k) He persistently infringes the Laws of the Game;

(l) He shows by word or action, dissent from any decision given by the Referee;

(m) He is guilty of ungentlemanly conduct.

For any of these three last offences, in addition to the caution, an **indirect free kick** shall also be awarded to the opposing side from the place where the offence occurred.

4. A player shall be **sent off** the field of play :

(n) If he is guilty of violent conduct, *i.e.*, using foul or abusive language, or if, in the opinion of the Referee, he is guilty of serious foul play ;

(o) If he persists in misconduct after having received a caution;

If play be stopped by reason of a player being ordered from the field for an offence without a separate breach of the Law having been committed, the game shall be resumed by an **indirect free kick** awarded to the opposing side from the place where the infringement occurred.

XIII.—FREE KICK

Free kicks shall be classified under two heads " direct " (from which a goal can

be scored direct against the offending side) and " indirect " (from which a goal cannot be scored unless the ball has been played or touched by a player other than the kicker before passing through the goal). When a direct or indirect free kick is being taken a player of the opposite side shall not approach within 10 yards of the ball until it is in play, unless he be standing on his own goal-line, between the goal-posts. If a player of the opposing team approaches within 10 yards before the kick is taken, the Referee shall delay the taking of the kick until the Law is complied with. The ball shall not be deemed in play until it has travelled the distance of its own circumference. The ball must be stationary when the kick is taken, and after taking the kick, the kicker shall not play the ball a second time until it has been touched or played by another player. In the case of a free kick being awarded to the defending side in the penalty area, the goalkeeper shall not receive the ball into his hands in order that he may thereafter kick it into play ; the ball must be kicked direct into play beyond the penalty area, and if this part of the Law is not complied with the kick shall be retaken.

Punishment. If the kicker, after taking the free kick, plays the ball a second time before it has been touched or played by another player, an indirect free kick shall be taken by a player of the opposing team from the spot where the infringement occurred.

XIV.—PENALTY KICK

A penalty kick shall be taken from the penalty mark and, when it is being taken, all players, with the exception of the player taking the kick and the opposing goalkeeper, shall be within the field of play, but outside the penalty area and at least 10 yards from the penalty mark. The opposing goalkeeper must stand (without moving his feet) on his own goal-line, between the goal-posts, until the ball is kicked. The player taking the kick must kick the ball forward ; he shall not play the ball a second time until it has been touched or played by another player. The ball shall be deemed in play directly it is kicked, *i.e.*, travelled the distance of its circumference, and a goal may be scored direct from such a penalty kick. If the ball touches the goalkeeper before passing between the posts, when a penalty kick is being taken at or after the expiration of half-time or full-time, it does not nullify a goal. If necessary, time of play shall be extended at half-time or full-time to allow a penalty kick to be taken.

Punishment.

(a) For any infringement by the defending team the kick shall be retaken, if a goal has not resulted.

(b) For any infringement by the attacking team, other than by the player taking the kick, the kick shall be retaken, if a goal has resulted.

(c) For any infringement by the player taking the penalty kick, a player of the opposing team shall take an indirect free kick from the spot where the infringement occurred.

XV.—THROW-IN

When the whole of the ball passes over a touch-line, either on the ground or in the **air**, it shall be thrown-in from the point

where it crossed the line, in any direction, by a player of the team opposite to that of the player who last touched it. The thrower, at the moment of delivering the ball, must face the field of play and part of each foot shall be either on or outside the touch-line. The thrower shall use both hands and shall deliver the ball from over his head. The ball shall be in play immediately it is thrown, but the thrower shall not again play the ball until it has been touched or played by another player. A goal shall not be scored direct from a throw-in.

Punishment.

(a) If the ball is improperly thrown-in the throw-in shall be taken by a player of the opposing team.

(b) If the thrower plays the ball a second time, before it has been touched or played by another player, an indirect free kick shall be taken by a player of the opposing team from the place wher the infringement occurred.

XVI.—GOAL KICK

When the whole of the ball passes over the goal-line, excluding that portion between the goal-posts, either in the air or on the ground, having last been played by one of the attacking team, it shall be kicked direct into play beyond the penalty area, from a point within that half of the goal area nearest to where it crossed the line, by a player of the defending team. A goalkeeper shall not receive the ball into his hands from a goal kick in order that he may thereafter kick it into play. If the ball is not kicked beyond the penalty area, *i.e.* direct into play, the kick shall be retaken. The kicker shall not play the ball a second time until it has touched or been played by another player. A goal shall not be scored direct from such a kick. Players of the team opposing that of the player taking the goal kick shall remain outside the penalty area whilst the kick is being taken.

Punishment. If a player taking a goal kick plays the ball a second time after it has passed beyond the penalty area, but before it has touched or been played by another player, an indirect free kick shall be awarded to the opposing team, to be taken from the place where the infringement occurred.

XVII.—CORNER KICK

When the whole of the ball passes over the goal-line, excluding that portion between the goal-posts, either in the air or on the ground, having last been played by one of the defending team, a member of the attacking team shall take a kick from within the quarter circle at the nearest corner-flag post, which must not be removed, *i.e.*, a corner kick. A goal may be scored direct from such a kick. Players of the team opposing that of the player taking the corner kick shall not approach within 10 yards of the ball until it is in play, *i.e.*, it has travelled the distance of its own circumference, nor shall the kicker play the ball a second time until it has been touched or played by another player.

Punishment. For an infringement of this Law an indirect free kick shall be awarded to the opposing team, to be taken from the place where the infringement occurred.